CRAFTSMAN CREATIVE

Written By
Daren Smith

craftsmancreativebook.com

For my wife, April, and our three awesome dudes,

You inspire me every day to be
a better husband and father.

Table of Contents

The Parable of The Contractor and The Craftsman

Once Upon a Time . . .

There was a Contractor and a Craftsman.

The Contractor has been building homes since they were a child. They learned from their father, a finish carpenter, who learned from their father. They've built homes the same way for decades. Their small business has had the same clients, the same size projects, and the same budgets for years. In fact, the business hasn't grown at all since the Contractor took over from their "Pop."

Every day is the same.

Every so often the Contractor reads a book or takes a course on "how to make more money building houses." They click on every ad that touts some "secret" or "shortcut" to riches. They often spend time late at night or early in the morning improving their craft. Their skillset is one-of-a-kind, and their business is known for some of the best detail work in the state. However, despite all of this, nothing seems to grow their business or improve their circumstances.

Work has slowed recently for the Contractor.

They were living month to month, but now things are even tighter, and the constant stress of needing more clients and projects keeps them up at night. There are economic and market realities that are out of their control—machines, for instance, that can do a similar job for lower cost. The price of materials has risen dramatically over the last year, too. The Contractor is worried for their partners and family. *What will I do if the business fails?* is a question that never leaves them.

"I must not be cut out for this," they say, sipping their drink before going on with their day.

Just as they did the day before.

The Craftsman

The Craftsman is a builder and a creative, too. They, on the other hand, came to this line of work after seeing a video on YouTube with millions of views of a person who built an entire cabin with their own two hands.

This video sparked something in the Craftsman. They were already a successful business owner—running a boutique marketing agency for more than a decade—but saw an opportunity to build tiny, off-the-grid homes for people who were looking to escape the city for some peace and quiet.

They sought out an investor who wanted to expand their real estate portfolio and partner on the purchase of a huge plot of land—hundreds of pristine, quiet acres perfect for tiny houses. They then found one perfect client and made them an offer the client couldn't refuse: their own little place, off the beaten path, at a price they could easily afford. Before the Craftsman had even broken ground, more than half of the plots were sold, and all the new owners had given her sizable deposits for the work. They now had more capital to put into the infrastructure and the design of the cabins, and they started talking with their investor about purchasing a second plot to accommodate the demand.

The Craftsman hired the best contractors to build the homes at a comfortable profit margin. Once the homes were sold, they split the money 50/50 with their investor partner.

With their marketing agency, the Craftsman spent most of their time working *in* the business, but with this new opportunity they're now spending most of their time working *on* the business, leveraging capital and labor to grow the business without needing to do the day-to-day work. The best part? They own 100 percent of the company. The more they grow the business, the larger the upside.

Most of their "work" now consists of managing the systems that they built.

- The system for finding new buyers.
- The system for building homes on time and under budget.
- The system for ensuring that the business takes care of their customers so that they refer their friends, which keeps the cost of acquiring a new client low.

Now the Craftsman is creating their next opportunity, which will bring them even more fulfillment and success in the years ahead. It's a lot of work, but they wouldn't choose anything else.

Now you may think that these are two separate people. But they're not. They're based on one person . . . me.

Photo by Stephanie Baker

In 2006, I started my first company, SoundSmith Studios, a boutique post-production sound services company. Things were great at the beginning. I started the business with a student loan that bought me a Mac Pro, a $1,200, 42-inch flat-screen TV, and a killer surround sound system. I thought the best equipment would make me better at my job.

My first paying gig was on a small independent feature. I still have a framed dollar bill from the literal bag of money that I was handed in a parking lot from one of the producers. He was a doorman at Sundance Resort and paid me in ones and fives, his tip money from the summer.

The business grew to where I was paying myself around $40k a year. I wasn't great at finding new clients (I had too much work to do!) and ultimately partnered with the director of that first feature to form a production company! Things were looking great, I thought. Yet, in about a decade of owning and running that business, I never paid myself more than $45k a year. In that time I got married, had three boys, and bought a home . . . suddenly that $45k had to stretch further and further each year.

At the end of 2017, I parted ways with that business and decided to take everything I'd learned over the previous decade of running my own businesses and do better this time.

I became a freelance film and TV producer. In the first year I made more than double what I'd ever paid myself in the past. And then I doubled my income the next year as well. I started leveraging other people's money for new projects, like a TV pilot, a short film teaser for a feature film, and documentary projects.

But then, the pandemic hit . . .and yet my income stayed the same! How could that be?

There's one reason, and one reason only. I had the same work ethic, so it wasn't that. I had about the same skill set, so it's not that either. I didn't have more money, more connections, or more resources . . .The only thing that changed was my mindset, and that mindset shift was the progression from thinking of myself and approaching my business like a contractor to thinking like a Craftsman.

Daren | Craftsman Creative 🏆 ···
@darentsmith

Information is not a value proposition anymore.

You can get all of the info & knowledge you need online for free.

So your value prop isn't "the secret".

It only can be your ability to help someone achieve a specific outcome.

1:00 PM · Aug 18, 2021 · Typefully

The more I thought about it in the hours and days that followed, the more I felt this *spark* that I needed to do something to support my belief—or, rather, to put up or shut up.

I'd been helping creatives through **courses** and **blogging** and **books** for years. But I'd never owned the outcome for them. I always just told them, "If you do the work . . . it works!" What if I could treat creatives like clients, even if no money had changed hands. What if I could do more to help them grow their businesses, reach more people, and make more money, not just by sharing more information, but joining them on their own creative journey and helping them grow their businesses?

What a challenge it would be to create a way to share ownership of the outcome! That excited me because it meant that if I succeeded then I could dramatically change the lives of the people I worked with!

But, what outcome? What was I trying to help creatives achieve, and how would I produce that outcome with them? More clients? More projects? More what? And how would we achieve it?

From that spark was born a new book—*The Craftsman Creative*.

The goal is to help you, dear reader, achieve the amazing goal of building a six-figure creative business. By following the chapters in this book, doing the work, and taking consistent action over a long enough period of time, that outcome will become inevitable. It's not just about the information in this book, but the actions you take as you gain insight after insight and apply the principles and frameworks to your business, starting with your mindset. Don't worry, I'm going to help you every step of the way.

I'm excited to be joining you on the journey ahead.

The 30,000-Foot View

The journey you'll take through this book and beyond . . .

I've added this chapter upfront because it's something I wish more books had—a 30,000-foot view of where we're starting and where we'll end up.

In this book I'm going to show you how to build a six figure, one person creative business.

And since, statistically, most people don't read every book all the way to the end, I want to lay it all out for you right here at the start. Here's everything you need to do to get that outcome:

- Find and connect with an audience of people
- Create a profitable, no-brainer offer
- Manually put that offer in front of your audience
- Manually sell that offer to a few people in that audience
- Automate putting the offer in front of your audience
- Automate selling it to your audience
- Optimize both to sell more
- Optimize the whole system for the amount of money, time, effort, and freedom you desire.

Of course there's nuance to each and every step in the process, but if you stop right here, you have enough *information* to create a successful, six-figure business for yourself. The nuance, and the *actions* to take, are what fill the rest of the pages you're about to read.

This book isn't just a book, it's part of a journey you're taking as the reader. But how did you learn that Craftsman Creative even existed and get here? Maybe it was via an ad on **Facebook**, or a **tweet**, or a **course**. Maybe you saw it after visiting my **website**, or joining the **email list**, or subscribing to the **newsletter**. Maybe you saw a link to the **book**, whether it was while it was being **written in public**, or after it was published.

What we're talking about here is roads to finding a business, product, or service. The same journey that others will walk to reach you and your business.

Once you've read and implemented what's in this book, you'll have all the information you need to go from a five-figure creator to a six-figure business owner and to bring others on the journey with you.

But that change doesn't come simply from the acquisition of knowledge.

It comes from action.

It's my goal to give you everything you need to start taking action and making the changes necessary to develop your business and reach that next level with your creative work. If you do the work, the process, principles, systems, and frameworks laid out in this book are a direct path to that desired outcome. If you don't do the work, I make no promises.

You're welcome to read the book all the way through first if that's what you prefer, but at a certain point you'll have to take the knowledge you've gained and begin practically applying it to your real-world business. As a creative, it can be hard sometimes to move from idea to action. You'll find tips for overcoming that tendency, and much more, in these pages.

This book is split up into six parts, and they are meant to be read in order. Like building a home, you start with the foundation, then frame in the walls, then lay sheets of plywood on the roof, then finish the exterior, then the interior. Here is our blue-print for a successful creative business.

Part 1 - Mindset Mastery

Part 2 - Vision and Goal Setting Mastery

Part 3 - Financial Mastery

Part 4 - Marketing and Audience Building Mastery

Part 5 - Sales Mastery

Part 6 - Leverage, Systems, and Growth Mastery

Each one of these parts represents an essential element of the business you're going to learn to build through this book. A very specific type of business: one that's resilient and profitable. One that can support your creative work for decades and that can withstand any shifts in the economy, your market, or your industry.

There's one thing missing from this business. Your product or service, which you already have.

This book isn't about creating SAAS businesses, startups, creative businesses, service businesses, drop-shipping businesses, or any other type of business. It's not about creating the best product, though the sections on Mindset Mastery, Marketing Mastery, and Sales Mastery may help you rethink your approach. Growing your business isn't about creating more or better art. **It's about shifting your mindset from thinking like a creator to thinking like a business owner.**

Write that one down. Put it in front of you. Look at it every day.

When the pandemic shut down the economy in the spring of 2020, events and concerts were shuttered. All of my musician friends were hurting, as their main source of income was turned off overnight. The default response from most of them was to focus on their *product*, the live music they performed for audiences.

Some went online and asked for donations through Venmo. Some put together small, intimate, outdoor concerts. Some stopped altogether.

The one constant was that none of them made any money. Except for those that focused on their *business* instead of their performance income.

Some of these creators decided to repackage their product in a different form like an **online course**. Some decided to write music intended for licensing to others. By focusing on their business, these individuals thrived through the pandemic.

In Part One, we'll focus on your mindset as a creator. You'll learn new ways to think about your work, the job(s) that people are hiring you for, and how to do that work at a professional level. You'll build new, mindful habits and routines that help you get into a peak state whenever you want, and snap out of negative states when you find yourself stuck there. You'll have a new perspective on your role in your business, and you'll learn the three personas every business owner needs.

In Part Two, we're going to look at your vision and goals. We'll create a vision for your future that pulls you out of bed each morning. This will serve as your north star as you build your new creative business: what you want your life to look like, what kind of work you want to be doing, and the reasons that you're driven to do that work for the people you seek to serve. We'll learn how to draft and adopt attainable goals, and explore sprints and other methods for accomplishing those goals. In Part Three, we'll learn the financial systems, frameworks, beliefs, and patterns that successful creators use to build and grow their businesses. Enough of the "starving artist" stereotype and the living paycheck to paycheck lifestyle. Let's create a profitable business with consistent cash flow. Let's create the confidence that you've set up your financial foundation for a successful business to be built upon.

In Part Four, we'll take a new look at marketing and audience building. Even if you "suck at marketing" (like I did in the past), you'll find ways to automate different parts of the process and get more awareness for the work you're doing.

A business without marketing is like a man winking in the dark. Only he knows he's doing it.

Having a marketing system that generates awareness and engagement for your business makes everything easier. You'll have more clients and customers, make more sales and revenue, and be able to grow your influence with people who want to be on the journey with you. You'll learn how to create superfans by delivering more value than anyone else can because you're the only one that can be you.

In Part Five, we'll look at sales and deals. You can double your business in this section alone.

Here are two quick examples.

I recently sat down to lunch with a friend who was building a business centered around investing. He was having a tough time getting the money he needed.

I asked him how the deals were structured and offered a new option. "Change the default investment. Instead of $2,500, make it $25,000."

His eyes lit up and he instantly messaged his business partner. That change alone will more than double their business and the amount of money coming in.

I recently spoke with another friend who was starting a podcast. She only had a single offer to bring in money for the business—sponsorships.

In our conversation, we explored different ways to monetize the information and the opportunities:

- Merch
- Courses
- Coaching
- Books
- Events

Thinking outside of the box a little helped her see a bigger, more sustainable (and profitable) business rather than a small content business built on a single revenue stream.

You will do the same for your business and you'll instantly be able to add more clients, more pricing tiers, and more offers to your business without requiring extra work or capital or people.

Lastly, in Part Six, after having built the foundation, the walls, the roof, and the exterior, we'll get into the details. We'll look at how to move from working harder to working smarter.. You'll learn to avoid the trap of linear thinking. You'll build systems to automate the parts of your business that you shouldn't be doing manually any longer. You'll learn to use leverage and reputation to close on more deals. And you'll begin planning for success, instead of chasing flawed baselines. We'll use all of these tactics to grow (if it makes sense for you).

I want to touch on an important point before we get started. The purpose of a business isn't necessarily to grow. That's not the ultimate goal of this book. The goal is to help you become a creative business owner of a profitable business and stay one as long as you desire.

If you want to grow, by the end of our time together here, you'll know how. But if you want to stop growing at a certain point and have a nice, consistent business that is arguably easier because the market dynamics are in your favor, then go for it.

Say you're a photographer. You currently make $50k a year shooting 35 weddings. You could try to grow to 52+ weddings a year, and you'd make more money. But you would burn out pretty quickly.

So you could hire other photographers and take a percentage of their sales, but now you're managing photographers rather than taking photos.

Another option is to systematize parts of your business so you make more profit per wedding, increase your pricing because you're creating more value, and limit the number of weddings you do per year, which decreases supply and increases demand.

Now you're charging $5k per wedding and limiting your workload to shooting 20 weddings a year. That's twice the income with close to half the amount of work, and it was achieved creatively via something other than "growing your business."

Learning to work smarter, not harder.

But I'm getting ahead of myself.

Let's start with that foundation.

PART 1

Mindset Mastery

*"Success is 80 percent mindset, only
20 percent strategy and skills"*
— Tony Robbins

A few years ago I was so frustrated that I wasn't where I wanted to be in my career yet. I was desperate to figure out why. I had worked so hard, at times putting in fifty- and sixty-hour weeks. I had devoted all of my spare hours to learning my craft and improving my skills. I took every gig I could. I sold my butt off. And I created good work.

Yet, still, I was stuck. I had no idea how to break through that $100,000 mark with my business. I didn't have anyone showing me the path, so it was trial and error after trial and error after trial and error. The result felt like a whole lot of nothing.

What I've learned in the years since is that there isn't one magic pill. Every author and influencer will try and tell you *their* way to help sell more books and get more followers, but the secret is that there is no *one* way for creators to find success.

There are, however, principles that have been tested and proven over time. One of the most important is the principle that starts this section on mindset: "success is 80 percent mindset, and only 20 percent strategy and skills." I learned that lesson the hard way, and I wish I'd internalized it a decade earlier. It's not about your talent, your skills, your tools, or your strategy. The biggest impact you can have on your business is to change your mindset—specifically, to stop seeing yourself as just an artist or creator, and start thinking of yourself as a business owner.

CHAPTER 1

The Three Personas Every Creative Business Needs

❖ ❖ ❖

Learn to tap into different personas
to grow your business

I started my first company while in college, doing live sound at local venues and post-production sound for film and television projects. I made around $35,000 that year between the summer of 2007 and 2008, which as a single college student was decent money! I was going to school and doing most of the projects at night or on weekends, so it worked out great. It was also one of the worst economic times in the United States, but I got through unharmed.

Ten years later, however, in 2017, I found myself with a wife and three young boys, a business partner, and a failing video production company. That year, with everything that happened in the business, I ended up paying myself about $36,000 . . . In ten years my financial situation objectively worsened. I was making less money (accounting for inflation) and had less of it to spend since my expenses had more than tripled. I needed to figure this whole business thing out, or else I wasn't going to be able to survive financially any longer.

This chapter outlines the most important mindset shift that every creative person needs to make in order to have a successful, long-lasting career doing what they love at a professional level.

To be clear, I mean making six figures a year doing what you love, without getting burnt out, and having the freedom and independence to live life in the way you want, whether that means growing a family, living in a certain city or country, or however you define freedom and independence for yourself.

The Three Personas Every Business Needs

In his book *The E-Myth Revisited*, author Michael Gerber outlines a few important mindsets that you need to apply to your creative business.

First, the fatal assumption:

That Fatal Assumption is: if you understand the technical work of a business, you understand a business that does that technical work.

Applying this to creatives, many make the fatal assumption that if they understand how to [create something], they understand a business that [creates that thing]. Yet, there are many filmmakers, writers, musicians, photographers, dancers, developers, freelancers, and more that are masters of their craft yet have struggling businesses.

Second:

The problem is that everybody who goes into business is actually three-people-in-one: The Entrepreneur, The Manager, and The Technician.

And the problem is compounded by the fact that while each of these personalities wants to be the boss, none of them want to have a boss.

So they start a business together in order to get rid of the boss. And the conflict begins.

If you're struggling in your business and feel stuck or frustrated or depressed by the current state of your business, or of your current life conditions, then it's likely because you're trying to run your business as a "technician." Using more applicable terminology, *you are trying to run your business as an artist.*

By doing so you are keeping the Entrepreneur and the Manager locked in the closet and have thrown away the key.

If you've ever said the words "I hate networking" or "I hate marketing" or "I suck at spreadsheets" or "I can't imagine having a schedule," then you've experienced this reality in your own business.

In order to succeed, you have to be three people in one. You have to, at strategic times, wear the hat of the Entrepreneur, the Manager, and the Artist.

The Mindset Shift That Matters Most: From Creator To Business Owner

Most likely you spend 90 percent of your time in one of three "personas" as I'll refer to them for the rest of this chapter and book.

Creators get stuck in the $50 to 80k yearly income range because they only ever use one persona to try and build their business. They, falsely, believe that the way to grow their business is to do more or better work. "If I could just get better at writing then I'd have a better business . . . "

Yet, there are plenty of below-average writers making six figures a year who have a thriving business. Same with founders who have a terrible idea but killer execution, a photographer who only uses trendy filters but is booked out for three months, or the YouTuber with much less experience than you with millions of subscribers and a new picture deal at Paramount. So the idea that "All you have to do is get better at your craft" can't be true, right? If it isn't true, then what is true?

What's true is that these below-average creators have figured out how to step into those other two personas. They think and operate at times like an entrepreneur, and at other times like a manager. And, not so surprisingly, they have successful businesses.

Now that you know what's really going on here, let's dive deeper into these different personas, and then explore how to strategically step into them to finally grow your business from five to six figures using the principles in this book.

The Entrepreneur Persona

The Entrepreneur is the visionary, the creative person, the one who spends most of their time thinking about the future. They are comfortable dealing with uncertainty and the unknown because, "dreams don't have to be feasible or have a plan!" "We'll get there somehow!"

There are good and bad traits to each of these personas that we need to cover so that we consciously choose the good traits and avoid the bad.

Imagine a successful businessman. Slicked back hair, thousand dollar shoes, three-piece suit, getting out of their blacked-out Tesla.

No doubt they parked in a handicap stall because they can do whatever they want the consequences can come if they dare.

Inside the office they expect adoration from their "subordinates," and demand control and attention wherever they strut.

They use that control to get what they want from their company at all costs. The only direction theyaccepts is "up and to the right," and if they knew what people said behind their back when they're out golfing or traveling, they'd fire those naysayers in an instant.

They command no real respect or influence other than what control they can hold in their grasp. But they're the visionary, so everyone just goes along with it while the gettin' is good. But they know that this state is fleeting and will ultimately come to an end, so they must take as much as they can now.

Gross, right?

These aren't traits you want to embody, and there are plenty of examples of visionary success without all of the icky, slimy stuff.

Take our other Entrepreneur. They discovered how to create solar charging technology that can be used anywhere, costs little, and serves starving communities all over the world.

They lead with vision and inspire people to join them in their mission to bring clean electricity to one billion people in their lifetime.

They're incredibly prolific and productive because every waking minute is spent on their mission, and people can see how authentic and inspiring they are by the way they live their life. Their confidence isn't bravado, but a quiet confidence that inspires others to be like them.

Ahh. That feels much better, doesn't it?

The qualities we want from the Entrepreneur persona are vision, quiet confidence, influence, humility, integrity, and leadership. It's not about what the business produces or does, but about the way the Entrepreneur approaches their work and those they work with.

For your business, the Entrepreneur persona will define the vision for your company and yourself. It will set big goals that feel in the moment inspiring, but to the artist and manager may feel impossible and unattainable.

You'll spend a little time as the Entrepreneur in the chapter about creating your vision. You will step into a different mindset and open yourself up to possibility and potential, and you'll create a vision that extends far beyond just yourself and your current circumstances.

Every business owner needs to spend some amount of time as the Entrepreneur so that a vision can be created for the future and the day-to-day work can be informed by that vision. The vision creates alignment in the business that makes these big goals attainable.

The Entrepreneur will be the one to create new opportunities, new connections and partnerships, new growth, and new ideas.

Without those, your business will stay just how it is now, as mine did for more than ten years.

The Manager Persona

The Manager persona is equally important to the growth and success of a creative business.

A goal without a plan is just a dream.

The Entrepreneur's goal, without the Manager's plan (and the Artist's execution), is just a dream, so spending 100 percent of your time as an Entrepreneur is just as limiting as spending 100 percent of your time as an Artist or Manager.

The Manager thrives with plans and systems and frameworks. Then they take those plans, systems, and frameworks and optimize them to perform at a peak level. They ensure that the day to day work is actually getting the business closer to reaching its goals.

They don't spend time thinking about big dreams and vision! No! They just want to make what they have now work as best as it possibly can.

If the Entrepreneur is the one who steps into a restaurant and starts chatting up the hostess, then the Manager is the one checking their watch because their reservation was for 6:00, they arrived at 5:50 and it's now 6:03, so this restaurant has a faulty system that someone needs to look at!

The Entrepreneur admires the ambiance, the Manager admires the efficiency, and the Artist admires the food.

Every business needs a manager because *businesses grow by doing more of what works and less of what doesn't.*

The Manager is the persona that determines, through observation and analysis, (two words you'll never hear an Entrepreneur or Artist use) what is and isn't working!

The Manager allows the Artist to focus more of their time on their craft and making the work that serves their clients and customers. They create systems and automation that do menial tasks more efficiently.

Every business, and *especially* every creative business, needs a Manager persona at times.

If you feel like "I'm just not a Manager!" Don't stress.

You're going to take your vision and start creating a plan and a mission and a goal in the coming chapters, and you'll consciously step into that Manager persona!

You're more capable than you have allowed yourself to believe, and it's time to start realizing the incredible potential you have inside you.

The Artist Persona

The last of the three "personas" that Michael Gerber talks about in his book is the Technician, but for our purposes, we'll use the term Artist.

The artist is the persona that creates the art, crafts the product, provides the service, and creates what the business delivers to its clients and customers.

Without the artist, there is no business.

Even if you have an amazing Entrepreneur and an equally amazing Manager, you'd have a lot of incredible goals and detailed plans but no action.

Who else has a parent or in-law who had an amazing idea decades ago that has since become somebody else's billion-dollar business?

(I have a relative who claims to have thought of the idea of pull-ups, the kid diapers that you pull up and down like underwear!)

To have a successful business, you need a great idea, a purpose-driven plan, and massive action! You need all three personas!

Without ever stepping into the Entrepreneur persona, you're stuck doing low-level work that never compounds and never grows beyond time for dollars.

That's the mode I was in as a freelance sound engineer and filmmaker. Our "big idea" was to charge more money. Very creative . . . Without the Entrepreneur's vision you'll be stuck doing work that has a limit to how much you can charge.

If you never step into the Manager persona, you have dreams but no plan to achieve them, so you end up doing all the work yourself and burning out because there are no systems or optimization or automation or leverage. You don't know why you aren't making more money, or aren't getting more clients, or bigger projects, because you never spend any time analyzing what's working and what isn't.

And, of course, a business without an Artist persona that shows up every day is a business with no product or service. You can manage the details for years and never make a dollar. Many startup founders find themselves in this position because they marry a great idea with a good plan, but the manager in them keeps wanting to optimize and perfect the product before ever showing it to the public.

They can spend years and tens of thousands of dollars and never ship anything, so the business goes under.

Seth Godin has written often about "shipping." Reid Hoffman famously said, "If you aren't embarrassed by the first version of your product, you shipped too late."

What they're saying, in effect, is that you have to let the Artist show up at some point, do the work, and put the thing you made out into the world.

But, if you spend *all* of your time as an Artist, you'll never grow your business. Without exception, the creators I know that have been stuck their entire careers making five-figure salaries are stuck because they never step into the Manager or Entrepreneur personas to grow their business.

Let's look at how to do just that in a practical way so that you can start doing this for your business today.

How to Operate As the Different Personas

The short version is that it comes down to scheduling.

Schedule time in your calendar each day, week, month, quarter, and year to ensure that you step into these different personas and do the work that each persona is best at.

Once a year and once a quarter, your Entrepreneur needs to take control of your business to think about the vision for the next period, the opportunities you want to create, the growth you want to experience, and the dreams you want to make a reality, just as you will do in the Vision chapter.

Every month and every week, your Manager needs to take control to go over financials, look at your sales and marketing systems, and observe what's working and what isn't.

And your Artist needs to show up every day to do the work as a professional, rather than as a hobbyist who plunks away a little here and a little there without ever building up a body of work, or showing your work with the world, or building momentum behind the work that you're creating.

But what is the specific work that these three personas need to do? In the following chapters we'll start to unpack those tasks by starting with further redefining our mindset.

CHAPTER 2

Defining and Understanding Mindset

Your mindset is the most important aspect of becoming and being a successful creator

At the heart of each of the three personas is a shift in the way one thinks about the creative work they do. In this chapter, we'll define what mindset is, why it matters, and why you should care about mastering it. Doing so will lay the foundation for everything else we're going to build on top of it to help you grow your business.

Let's dive in!

First, what's mindset and why is it important?

Mindset is a set of beliefs, rules, dreams, and desires that live in your head that determine your thoughts, emotions, and actions.

Dictionary definition: A state of mind or attitude.

For our purposes, we'll look at mindset as *something that impacts the experiences in your life,* not just a state of mind or attitude. Extending the definition to include this will help you see how important your mindset is when it comes to reaching your goals and achieving your dreams.

Your mindset is important because it's what determines how you think, how you act, and how you feel every day. The quickest way to change how you feel is to change your mindset.

For example, if you *believe* that life is a gift, that influences the way you feel, the way you treat others, the emotions of gratitude that permeate your day-to-day life experience. If you can adopt that mindset, you can see how it translates to a better life experience.

Alternatively, if you believe that life is a *competition*, *test*, or *battle*, you'll have a very different life experience! You'll constantly be seeking out the rules. You'll wonder if others are cheating. You'll try and win and see life as a zero-sum game.

Can you already begin to sense and feel the differences in tension caused by those two opposing mindsets? The first feels open, easy, free, and beautiful. The other feels tense, charged, and on the verge of something bad.

Exploring that further, here's how your mindset ultimately affects how you feel every day.

Your Mindset Determines Your Thoughts

Let's say you get a phone call from an old friend. There's no inherent meaning in that phone call, except for the meaning you give it.

If you see life as a gift, you might get excited that your friend is calling you out of the blue! What an amazing blessing to be able to reconnect and catch up! If you see life as a game to be won, you might think that this person wants something or has some ulterior motive.

Nothing changed in this scenario except your mindset.

Now, extrapolate that out over hundreds of days, thousands of interactions, and you can see wildly different futures for these two different examples.

Your Mindset Determines Your Actions

How you respond to the person on the other end of a random phone call is informed by your mindset. That is, your mindset, framed by your thoughts, then informs your actions.

What you think is acceptable, or appropriate, or expected of you is part of your mindset. If you see a random phone call as an opportunity, you'll act differently than if you see it as a competition or a game to be won.

What if, instead of a phone call from an old friend, we were talking about a sales pitch to a potential client? Or a partnership with another creator? Or handling a customer's problem with your product?

Extending those actions over thousands of interactions across thousands of people will have a dramatic effect on your outcome.

Your Mindset Determines Your Feelings

Here's the real trick. By breaking down how we build our mindset, we can reverse engineer the mindset we want and need for success.

Your thoughts and actions are *inputs*, things that you create and do. They are internally motivated and completely in your control. Your feelings, on the other hand, are *outputs*. They are impacted by external forces and often feel outside of your control. They are determined by the *inputs* given at any particular moment.

If your mindset isn't optimized for the output you want, then you get something that looks like this:

Bad mindset + bad thoughts + bad actions = bad feelings.

But, if you change your mindset a little bit, you get:

Okay mindset + okay thoughts + okay actions = okay feelings.

And if you master your mindset, you get:

Incredible mindset + *empowering* thoughts + *massive* action = *extraordinary* feelings.

Think about that for a moment. If your day-to-day experience is one of suffering, frustration, or disappointment, you'll likely find yourself in a place that's very hard to grow, contribute, and create from. But what would your life be like if you felt *extraordinary* every single day? How would your work be impacted? How would your business change and grow? The obvious answer is that your life would be dramatically affected by this simple shift in mindset.

Here's what's amazing about this "equation" we've laid out. It's less of a straight line and more of a loop:

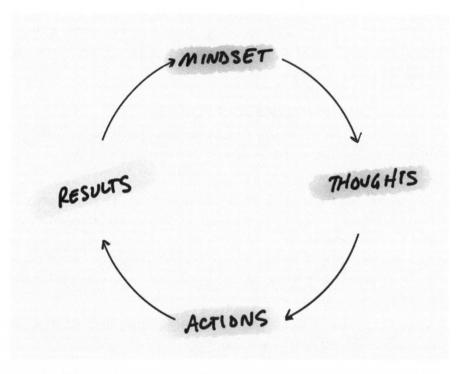

It's all interconnected and funnels from one stage to the next. If you can change your mindset to one of gratitude, faith, and abundance, you'll reap the results of a better emotional state and a stronger ability to do the creative work you desire.

One of the most important things I will do in this book is to show you that mindset comes first. Mastering it makes everything easier. It's our strongest path to becoming more creative, more influential, and more successful as business owners.

In the next chapter, we'll dive deeper into the feelings and emotional states that result from having a better mindset. How exactly does your emotional state impact the work that you do? By improving your emotional state, everything you touch gets better—your work, your life experience, your relationships, your health . . . everything.

CHAPTER 3

Take Control of Your Emotional States

Once you understand where emotional states come from, you can understand how to control them

We need to take a quick step back to understand where our emotions come from. In the last chapter, we learned that emotions are *outcomes*, so if we can control the inputs then we can better control the outcomes.

Emotions result from three things, our focus, our language, and our physiology.

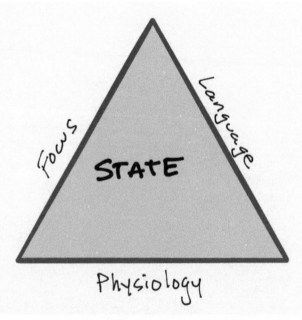

From Tony Robbins

At this point, put away any other distractions, and fully focus on the rest of this chapter. It's a lot to take in all at once and is only mastered after a *lot* of practice.

Emotion Comes from Physiology

Think about someone who is discouraged.

What do they physically look like? Slumped over, head down, shallow breathing, sullen face, right? At least that's how we often picture them. Now, what about someone who is confident? Standing upright, shoulders back, slight smile, big eyes, deep breaths.

That visual difference might seem fairly obvious. But when we take it one step further and apply this idea to our own physiology, that's where things get interesting.

I want you to create a confident emotional state using just your physiology.

Stand up. Stretch out your arms. Make yourself physically bigger. Take a few deep breaths. Put a "knowing smile" on your face, like you've got some secret that you can't wait to tell the world about. Stand confidently. Make fists with your hands and put them on your hips. Stand like Wonder Woman or Superman.

Now hold this pose, take deep breaths, and keep that smile on your face.

Do this for at least a minute, ideally two.

05 - Superman | Photo by King Lip on Unsplash

What you just experienced is the power of just *one* part of the "triad" that determines our emotions. Amy Cuddy spoke about the power pose in a **TED talk** a few years ago. It's absolutely worth a watch. How do you feel when you embody this position? Confident, right?

Let's quickly look at the other two parts of the triad to get the most out of this exercise.

Emotion Comes From Focus

Another common saying from the man who I learned all this from is "what you focus on is what you feel." I was at a Tony Robbins event in 2019 when I learned this lesson in a way that I'll never forget. Tony was working with a woman who, minutes before, had stood up and confided that just a few days ago she had contemplated taking her own life. Tony worked with her for more than an hour. At the beginning of their time together, you could see her physiology and hear the language she was using.

Her triad - her focus, physiology, and language—was causing her to feel like she wasn't enough, that she was worthless, and that things were never going to get better. She was suffering.

About halfway through their time discussing her situation, I saw her perspective start to shift. She had family members who loved, adored, and looked up to her. She had a gift for lifting others up and serving people. She had a reason that she was here on earth and a deep faith in God that kept her going. This light came into her eyes, and by the end of her conversation with Tony she was cheering, jumping up and down, and filling the entire room with joy.

The craziest part is what happened a few hours later. Another man stood up and said he, too, was thinking about taking his life. Rather than working with him one on one, Tony brought the woman over to help. She went from focusing on her own suffering to focusing on saving another person she had never, before that moment, even met. Talk about a mindset shift! All from a simple shift in focus from how bad things were, to how much she had to offer others in her world, a belief that she "was enough" and that she "was loved."

What we focus on is what we feel.

To best understand this, think about a child between the ages of five and ten. When something happens to them, they fixate on it. The smallest word or action can cause a storm of emotions that boils up into a full-blown *temper tantrum!*

Even my three boys—who are perfect little angels, of course— have these moments.

The reason these temper tantrums happen is that a child gets so focused on how they were wronged and how that makes them feel that they keep ping-ponging back and forth between the affront and the feeling until it all escalates and ultimately explodes.

Just the other day my youngest boy stormed into the room as if someone had decapitated his stuffed dog. "BUT HE STOLE MY TOY!" my seven-year-old yelled, tears streaming down his eyes.

His brother had picked up a Lego that the youngest had built—in our house, if you leave a toy alone for some time, it becomes fair game for someone to play with. "Stole" was an intense word for the situation, and it revealed what he was focused on, what had happened to *him*.

"Yes, but is that a good reason to hit someone?" I calmly replied.

"HE STOLE MY TOY!"

And on and on. They even tell you, loudly, that they are focused on one thing, and one thing only. If only they were able to see things from a different perspective . . .

The same happens in our adult lives. (Admit it, you have little temper tantrums, too.) We fixate on what someone said or did, or the economy, or the pandemic, or the industry, or our competitor. We focus on it and focus on it until it stirs us up into a ball of *emotions*.

You've likely experienced this in the last week. Maybe even today.

And it's not just bad emotions, either, that can take us over. Have you ever gotten so excited by a project that you worked yourself up into a fever and kept going without a break, until you realized it was midnight?

It's because we get so focused that we get into a sort of *flow*, where the only thing we can think of is the work in front of us. Who needs lunch, anyway? (Your kids do. They need lunch. Hurry, go feed them!)

But this knowledge provides an opportunity for empowerment. If you believe that you can control what you focus on, then you can start to control your emotions using this tool (directing your focus) just as you did with physiology (striking the Power Pose).

Want to get meta? What were you doing earlier when you were using physiology to change your state? You were focusing your thoughts on your current state and then making conscious changes. Mind blown yet?

Emotion Comes from Language

The words you choose and the way you use them affect your emotional states just as much as focus and physiology.

When someone hurts you, how do you respond?

You could say, "You're dead, I'm gonna kill you!" Or you could say, "Ooh. Sheesh, that hurt a little! Please don't do that!"

One is *very* emotionally charged (not to mention an outright threat), while the other is almost a little playful!

Say a client decided to go another way and work with a competitor. You could say: "That's it. I'm a failure. I'm worthless. I'll never succeed . . . " Or you could say: "Shucks. That's unfortunate, but I get it. Oh well!"

Can you *feel* the difference in just the language?

Look at the default words you use when good things happen and when bad things happen. How can you change the words you use to "soften the blow" when bad things happen, and "heighten the experience" when good things happen?

It's just as impactful to celebrate a huge win by saying, "Cool. probably a fluke. I'm not getting my hopes up that it happens again . . . " as it is by saying, "This is *incredible*! I'm so *grateful*!"

These are powerful ways to change your emotional state in an instant, if you choose to use them. They can help ensure that you stay in peak states more often and for longer periods of time, and can help you avoid feeling down and out because you're in a bad emotional state. These tactics have helped me tremendously, and the more that I practice them, the quicker I can snap out of emotional states that prevent me from showing up and doing my best work.

Now, one note. Just because you experience bad emotional states doesn't make *you* bad. We all experience times of distress. It just means that you have patterns that are creating those states, patterns that can be adjusted and changed. Please don't feel that you've failed or that you're not enough. Please don't get stuck in states of suffering. The point is to identify that it's happening and make new choices to change things for the better.

Determine the Most Important Emotional State for You

When you think about that time that you were in flow, feeling at the top of your game, what *was* the emotion you were experiencing?

Is that a constant for you? When you're in the zone, do you always experience *that* feeling? Are there other emotions that come with that feeling of being unstoppable and showing up as your best possible self?

If so, I want you to write those down.

When I'm in my peak state, I feel like my body can't keep up with my mind. Ideas flow so quickly, and it takes everything I have to capture them in time. In this state, time isn't a consideration. I could start at 9 am. Then, before I know it, it's 5 pm and I haven't taken a break to eat or use the bathroom or get some fresh air and sun. I crave these moments because I know that I'm serving and contributing at the highest level. I'm in the zone, so to speak, a place of peak creativity and clarity of thought. Clarity, for me, is one of the most empowering things—the more I understand something, the better I can use it. As we go through the next chapters, the emotions you wrote down to describe your peak state are the emotions that you're going to optimize for throughout your day. By continually finding your way back to those states, you'll cultivate a mindset for success. For instance, when I ask people what they feel when they're at their peak state, many answer, "happy." How, then, can one find their way to the feeling of "happy" in order to maximize their return to their peak state? By focusing on being happy. If you want to feel motivated, focus on feeling motivated. If you want to feel creative, focus on a time where you were insanely creative, in a state of pure flow. Use your focus, your language, and your physiology to get back into that state again and again.

There Is an Equation for Happiness

Tony Robbins—whose work in psychology and other areas has inspired much of this chapter—shares what he calls the equation for happiness. It's a very simple if/then equation:

$$LE = Life\ Experience \qquad EX = Expectations$$

$LE = EX$	$\longrightarrow$	😐
$LE < EX$	$\longrightarrow$	🙁
$LE > EX$	$\longrightarrow$	🙂

If your life experience = your expectations, you're satisfied.

If your life experience < your expectations, you're frustrated, or angry, or depressed.

If your life experience > your expectations, you're happy!

While it's simple, it's also incredibly powerful.

There's one side of this equation that's *much* easier to control than the other. Guess which? Exactly. It's easier to control our expectations, than our actual experiences. That's why it's so important to put focus on shifting what we're experiencing (i.e., the point of this chapter) to change our mindset.

Our expectations—the way we think things *should* be—can be adjusted at any moment. We can stop expecting our clients to act a certain way. We can stop feeling like the market owes us work, jobs, income, projects, etc. We can adjust our expectations of our audience. You can literally do any of those things right now.

If there is something in your business that's frustrating or stressful? Take a minute to identify the expectation you have around it.

For example, say you have clients who aren't paying on time. I've been there. It's frustrating! But can you change your expectation to one of gratitude for the work in the first place?

If not, then can you change the life experience to better match your expectation (prompt payment)? What can you change about the way things are? Maybe you can create a more rigid payment window, or get paid half of the budget upfront, or not deliver the final version until you've been paid in full?

Those are all examples of changing the life conditions, but they take longer and are harder to implement. If you want *instant* happiness, change (or lower) your expectations.

Now, let's take a step back.

We want to implement all of this emotional stuff at once because the better our mindset is, the better we will be at creating and showing up as our best selves. It's that "best self" that will do the work that inspires, influences, and changes people. The best self is the one who will grow your business. The best self is more likely to get paid in full on time.

Practicing control over your physiology, focus, and language will help you step into that best self more frequently and easily.

So that's what we need to do. Practice. Work at catching yourself when you're using unhelpful language. Take a break every hour to look at and adjust your physiology. Notice where your focus is and consciously choose to redirect it where you want it to be throughout the day.

There's no "done" with this process. It's ongoing, and you'll only get better at making these adjustments with time. But you'll never stop doing it because it's that important. Part of making any time of practice successful is supporting it with a proper foundation. That's why morning routines are so important. They can start us off in a peak state and have us diving into our work as our best selves.

CHAPTER 4

Morning Routines and Priming

*Your morning routine is your secret weapon
to a productive and effective day*

It's time to transition from theory to principles and actions that we can put into action. In the coming chapters, we'll cover some helpful mindsets and beliefs that will guide you through the other sections of this book, which focus on more practical elements of building a six-figure creative business.

Remember that your mindset is the foundation that you'll build your successful business on. Without that you'll risk having an unsteady foundation full of cracks that won't be able to hold the business you want to build on top of it.

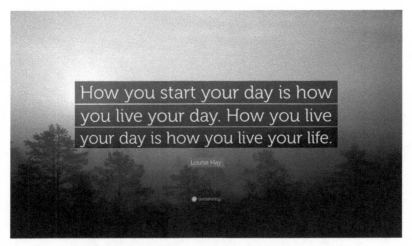

How you start your day is how you live your day. How you live your day is how you live your life.

Louise Hay

From QuoteFancy.com

Don't just skip past that quote. Read it again if you need. Really ponder it.

Our life is made up of days that are made up of moments. The consistent things that we do each day compound over time and create the life that we live.

If you want to change your *emotions*, you change the *inputs* of what you focus on, your physiology, and language. If you want better days, look at how they start.

It's easy for me to wake up early. I'm a morning person. But it's not just about the time of day; it's about the order of your day. A morning routine is simply the handful of things that you do between the time you wake up, and the time you start your day.

Now, there was a time when I didn't have a morning routine. I didn't understand how powerful they were, so I would sleep until the last minute (often silencing the alarm multiple times before that), slide out of bed, throw on a clean shirt (at least one that I couldn't smell from across the room), and head out in the nick of time to avoid being late.

That would describe most of my high school and college experiences. I even made the mistake once of signing up for a class in college that started at 7:00 am! What was I thinking?!

Only in the last two years or so that I realized the power a personalized morning routine has in creating the life you want for yourself and your business. I've since used my mornings to write books, work out and get in shape, or just have time alone every day.

I now see morning routines as a direct path to a handful of very clear outcomes, all of which fall under the umbrella of starting my day off with momentum. It's a conscious routine that gets me to *feel* a specific way every morning, so I can start my day the way I want to. I'll share what my current morning routine looks like at the end of the chapter. Until then, let's talk about a few emotions, or *outcomes*, that we can obtain through a morning routine.

- Gratitude
- Clarity

- Inspiration
- Energy
- Vision
- Solitude
- Confidence

Done properly, the morning routine brings these emotions, which provide the momentum to start your day, right to you. But how do we build a routine? What should we include and why? Where should we start? Here are some ways you can achieve those emotions and outcomes.

Gratitude Through Prayer

If you believe in God or are religious, you can substitute prayer for any sort of gratitude practice.

I start off my mornings by waking up, leaving my bedroom, and heading to the living room with my water bottle, phone, and AirPods. I kneel down on the couch and spend some time conversing with God. Most of the prayer is centered around gratitude—for my life, my family, my home, my friends, my experiences, my health, whatever comes to mind.

It's not a rote, repeated prayer. It's a conversation where I focus my thoughts around how much I have to be grateful for and share those thoughts with my creator. If I feel the need for help or guidance, I'll also ask during that prayer, and wait to see—or even *feel*—if an answer comes.

I follow this up as much as possible with time spent reading in the scriptures, which is where I often receive the answers that I'm asking for.

Clarity Through Meditation

After listening to hundreds of podcasts where top performers in different fields were interviewed, and hearing that so many have a meditation practice, I started to meditate consistently a few years ago.

The most simple description of meditation is time spent allowing your brain to calm down and let everything just pass you by.

We all have so much on our minds at all times—we're creatives, after all—that it helps our minds to relax and rejuvenate if we just take twenty or thirty minutes to let it all go and find some peace and calm.

Meditation has become a non-negotiable part of my morning routine, and my current streak is years long. If I somehow miss it in the morning, I'll find time as early in the day as possible to do a meditation so that I keep that streak going.

I use an app because the trigger of those specific sounds and having a guided meditation helps me to get to that place more quickly and easily. Currently I use the Oak meditation app and have used Calm and Headspace in the past.

Inspiration Through Journaling

In Julia Cameron's classic book *The Artist's Way*, she recommends a process she calls morning pages. These are three, free-hand, unedited pages of pure stream of consciousness that you write before your day gets going. It's an opportunity for your brain to get everything out and make room for new ideas and inspiration to occur. If you're an artist who creates on a regular basis and ever find yourself stuck or blocked, morning pages are the answer.

It's similar to what artists like Ed Sheeran and Neil Gaiman talk about, as shared in this thread: https://twitter.com/Julian/status/1402356373648601089?s=20. (Especially check out Ed Sheeran in the video in the thread talking about the process of "clearing out the tap of [crappy] water so that the clean water can flow.")

Beyond that, a journaling practice, where you write down what's on your mind, capture what happened during your day, and your hopes and dreams for the future is a helpful practice in a similar way. It creates space for new thoughts, ideas, and connections to occur.

Grab a notebook, or an app like **Day One**, and write away!

Energy Through Breathing and Exercise

I don't have time in this book to expand on the benefits of exercise, so I'll leave that to the experts, but I do believe strongly that exercising at least three times a week is essential to maintaining health and vitality. Every creative should have something—running, biking, swimming, hiking, lifting weights—that they do to keep their body healthy and strong.

On days that I don't exercise, I make sure to take time to at least stretch and do some breathing exercises. Bringing in air, expanding the lungs, feeling my body, and getting moving are all important ways for me to wake up physically as well as mentally.

A helpful breathing exercise that I've used for a while now is to breathe in a 1:4:2 ratio. For example, breathe in for 4 seconds, hold for 16 seconds, exhale for 8 seconds. Do this 10 times and you'll instantly feel more awake and alert.

Vision Through Priming

Priming is just what it sounds like: getting my mind and body ready for action.

I use a YouTube video every morning that helps me prepare for the day ahead and visualize what I want to accomplish. It helps me focus and build excitement around the day ahead so that I can't wait to get started.

If you find yourself starting your workday sluggish and unmotivated, priming is something I would look at adding to your morning routine.

Two other things you can incorporate into your morning routine:

SOLITUDE

If you are married or spend a lot of time around other people, it can be helpful to have at least 15 minutes in the morning to yourself. Make a cup of coffee or tea or hot chocolate (or my favorites, **Crio Brü** or **MUD\WTR**) and have some time to yourself to do whatever you want before others wake up.

WATER

Arguably the simplest, single thing you could do to start your day off better is to chug some water right when you wake up. My wife and I both have 40-ounce insulated water bottles that never leave our side. It just sits there on the floor waiting for me to wake up. I'll drink at least 8 to 10 ounces before I even get all the way out of bed, and use it to kick off my morning routine.

Crafting Your Own Morning Routine

Your morning routine will require a personal journey of experimentation to land on what works best for you.

If you don't currently have a morning routine, start small. Pick the emotions or outcomes covered in this chapter that matter most to you, and start there, with just one or two. You can add more along the way.

If you have a morning routine that's working for you, consider being even more intentional about the outcomes that you're trying to get from that routine. That will help you focus and get those outcomes even quicker and easier, potentially allowing for more practices to become part of your morning.

Don't stress over this. There's no right answer. There's no correct amount of time you need to spend. You won't be graded or judged by having a routine that looks completely different than mine.

I like having hours of time to myself each morning. If I get less than an hour, I feel rushed and not in control of my day, so I tend to get up early (generally between 5:30 and 6:30, depending on how late I was up the night before) to allow for my whole morning routine, uninterrupted.

Others can get up, stretch, make a cup of coffee, and are ready to go.

Yours will be yours. Perfectly suited to you and your needs.

My Current Morning Routine

I'm sharing mine here not as a measuring stick or for comparison, but for inspiration. Steal anything that you want, change it up, make it work for you if you need a jumping-off point.

6:00-6:30 am - Wake up (using a wake-up window created in the **Sleep Cycle app**), drink water, use the bathroom, brush my teeth) Update: since writing the first draft of this chapter, I've started waking up naturally. Some days that's 5:30 or even 5:00 am, but most days it's between 6:30 and 7:15am.

15 to 20 minutes - Prayer, focused on gratitude

30 minutes - Scripture study

20 minutes - Meditation, using the **Oak app**

20 minutes - Priming, using this video on **YouTube**

30 minutes - Exercise, using the **X3 bar** at home.

20 minutes - Shower and ready

20 minutes - Make breakfast for my wife and kids

Roughly 9:00 am - Start my workday, generally with a deep work session with **Brain.fm** as background music

I included all the way through to the workday so you can see how the morning routine flows into the beginning of work.

The outcomes are all present by the time I'm making breakfast for the family, and I'm in a great emotional state that—I believe, at least—helps my family with the start of their day. If I'm happy, they tend to default to happy as well.

There's a ton of privilege that I haven't addressed here. I have all of this time every day, uninterrupted. I have a wife who helps get the kids ready and takes them to school. I work from home, so I don't have a commute. Not everyone has the same situation, so please understand, again, that this isn't some standard you are going to be held to.

This is my experience, and I'm lucky and blessed and grateful because of it. If you are frustrated that you don't have the same amount of time or the same freedom in your circumstances, don't be. Use what you learned in the last chapter to take control of your morning, your time, your day. It may not look the same, but you can absolutely take control more than you think you can.

The compounding effect of doing that routine day after day leads to a very different destination after weeks, months, and years of daily practice.

CHAPTER 5

Success Requires Faith

Everything about mindset leads to one truth:
success requires faith

In this chapter, we'll look at what faith is, why it's required, and how to gain more faith as you move forward in building a six-figure creative business. Faith is a foundational part of our mindset as it shapes what is possible, how we approach the work we do and our day to day lives, and it affects how we see the world around us. Resilience comes from faith. Grit comes from faith.

In 2008 I was a "sound guy" who had partnered with a director/editor to make commercials, and someday movies, together. In 2008-2009 we wrote our first screenplay together, and quickly realized we needed someone to help us get funding to turn that screenplay into a movie.

Not knowing any producers, my business partner suggested that I take the job. He had incredible faith in me, which led to me transitioning out of being a sound guy to being a full-time producer by 2012. By 2018 I was making six-figures a year as a producer, and in 2021 I finally, after 12 years, produced my first feature film. That faith he had in me led to me having faith in myself, and that faith led to more than a decade of persistence and resilience to simply stay in the game long enough and keep trying time and time again until it all worked out. As I write this in October of 2021, I already have three projects lined up to produce in 2022, and know that I will make six figures before the year even starts. Faith pays off.

Faith is Belief + Action

This is the best definition I've been able to come up with to describe faith.

There are many scriptural definitions that could also work, but for those that didn't grow up studying scriptures, the leap may be too great to use those definitions here. (Though, if you want a deep dive on faith, you can **read this chapter** in a book of scripture called The Book of Mormon)

Faith, in the scriptures, is what leads to miracles. There is immense power in faith. What we want to do is channel that faith into action that benefits our clients and customers as well as our business.

Replace Your Limiting Beliefs With Empowering Beliefs

We need to look deeper at the two parts of that definition of faith.

Belief is a feeling of certainty or confidence about something, an acceptance that something is true. Beliefs, unlike facts, don't need to have any tangible evidence or proof in order to be held. You can believe in ghosts, or aliens, or conspiracy theories, or God, or any number of things. But, for our purposes, we need to look at the beliefs that you hold about yourself and your business.

Sitting here now, reading this book, do you believe that you will succeed?

On a scale of 1-10, how would you rate your level of certainty or confidence? Until you are at an 8 or above in your belief, your disbelief in yourself is going to be a major obstacle.

Think about how you learned to ride a bike. At some point, you had to believe that the weird combination of balance and momentum would prevent you from falling over. So you kept trying and trying until you succeeded. But you needed that belief to get there and move beyond your fear of falling or feeling of being frustrated or stuck.

There is no evidence at the start that your business is going to work. There is no guarantee. In fact, most businesses fail. If you believe that your business is like most, then you're setting yourself up for more work—the hard work you'll need to succeed and the work you'll have to do against your own limiting beliefs. You have to give them up and let them go. (Or, if you prefer a more intense visual, burn them to the ground!)

You're a smart person, as evidenced by the fact that you are reading this book.

And as we've seen in previous chapters, you can change your focus, your language, and your emotion in a moment. So why would you continue believing that you aren't going to succeed? Are you waiting for someone else to have that belief for you? Because that's not going to happen. (When has it ever?) Are you waiting for some proof or evidence that you are going to succeed? Because that doesn't exist either.

Every day of your business is going to take faith and the belief that you will succeed despite all odds, and that you are the person to lead this business to that success.

What beliefs would help you do better work every day, feel more confident about your work, and motivate you to keep pushing forward? Why not switch out the limiting beliefs for those awesome beliefs?

Try it now. Think of the most limiting belief you have.

Generally, it starts with "I can't because . . . "

For years, I'd attend family gatherings and people would ask me how the producing thing was going. My answer would inevitably include something like, "well, we just need some money," or "the industry isn't producing much independent film right now." Those were my limiting beliefs. They were out of my control, yet I let them dictate my actions and my potential for success. What is your "I can't because . . . ?" That's the belief I want you to think about and hold in your mind right now.

Now, ask yourself: is that really true? If you still believe it is, ask this follow-up: what evidence do you have to support that

"I can't because" statement? And if you can't find any evidence, then why would you continue to believe that limiting belief?

Now you can finally release yourself from being held back by that belief and replace that thought with a new, empowering belief.

Try it now! Take one of the new beliefs that would help motivate and inspire you and repeat it aloud, write it down, repeat it multiple times a day until it becomes your new default answer.

"My business is going great because [new belief]!"

Doesn't that feel so much better?

Beliefs Without Action Will Get You Nowhere

Now that we have these empowering beliefs, we need to turn them into action.

There was a period of a few years where my actions weren't supporting my beliefs. You could say my faith was lacking. I was too focused on my limited beliefs, and I stopped taking action. In years past I'd gone out to LA for the American Film Market (AFM) each November to meet with producers and sales agents about the movie I was trying to get produced. Now my limiting beliefs (and the lack of money to make the trip) had crept in and stopped me from attending (or believing that I could still make movies). It wasn't until I took on a gig producing a TV show in 2018 that my faith was renewed. I was able to see how good I was as a producer, and I started pursuing movie production again. Surprisingly, it wasn't a movie that I'd written or found that I ended up producing. Two other people who I'd been working with saw the action that I was taking to produce a feature and asked if I would come and produce their movie.

Derek Sivers' books have mentored me in so many ways. I will never be able to thank him enough. He wrote an incredible blog post about this topic, which you should read, called **Ideas are just a multiplier of execution.**

Sivers shows that even the best ideas (or beliefs) matched with weak or no execution (or action) have nothing on a weak idea matched with brilliant execution. The best combination, however, is to pair the most empowering beliefs and ideas with brilliant execution, which will inevitably succeed. The reason I add inevitably is that if you choose to be resourceful, determined, and never give up, that in and of itself is a success.

One book that I read every year is Think and Grow Rich by Napoleon Hill. It's a financial classic that's been read by millions of people. One of the most impactful passages from my latest reading of the book is this:

One of the most common causes of failure is the habit of quitting when one is overtaken by temporary defeat.

Ninety-nine percent of people either never try (lack of action) or give up at the first sign of defeat (lack of empowering beliefs).

That's why these two together are so important.

Belief + action = faith.

And faith is what is required to succeed.

Do this today—change your beliefs to empowering ones and commit to taking action no matter what. Keep going, make progress every day on your goals and your business, and you will inevitably succeed. You will have goals that you don't achieve, but your beliefs will help you set new goals, raise your standards, and take action. There will be hard times, but your faith will help you get through them. Your faith is 100 percent in your control; no one can give it to you or take it away. The more you protect it, nurture it, and rely on it, the further it can take you in your life and your business.

Start each day with faith—use your morning routine to reinforce that faith and give you the momentum to take action every day. Over time, you'll see how much of an impact dedication to belief and action can make on your progress and your growth.

PART 2

Vision and Goal Setting Mastery

"If you don't know where you are going, you will probably end up somewhere else."
— Lawrence J. Peter

Returning to our parable—and remembering that both the Contractor and the Craftsman are, in fact, me and you—it's important I share my story throughout this book so that you don't think the path from creative to business owner is an easy one or a linear one. Reality is rarely linear. Life is full of setbacks, frustrations, doubts, and discouragements. But every so often there are periods of massive change and growth where the dreams we're working toward feel like they're within reach if we keep going.

Mindset mastery has been one of the most important pursuits the last few years. In 2019 I was really down, despite having an incredible marriage, three loving and healthy boys, a house, and making more money than I ever had before. It was these down months that motivated me to attend the Date with Destiny seminar with Tony Robbins in December 2019, where I learned so much about myself and about how life works. That experience provided a pivot point for me and my career. I gained so much clarity and came out of it with so much more gratitude, a greater sense of purpose, and a desire to contribute to the lives of others who were struggling as I had.

One of the biggest shifts you can make as a creative or artist is to begin seeing yourself as a business owner. Start with understanding and inhabiting the three personas and becoming mindful of your mindset and how you're showing up every day. Shifting your mindset alone isn't enough. You have to add faith. You have to keep going despite how hard it can be at times.

It took me more than twelve years to produce my first feature film, with a director and production company that I'd worked with for more than two years prior to being hired on the movie. Twelve years!

I'd experienced an unsuccessful exit of a company that I'd helped build for more than nine years, a short stint in 2009 where I had to leave the industry to sell cars just to stay afloat and pay for my life with my new wife, and a string of unsuccessful screenplays and TV pilots and pitches. How was I able to keep going after all that? It's because I had a set of beliefs – a mindset – that I would never give up. To me, success boiled down to a matter of time and effort, mixed with a little bit of luck and a lot of grace.

Throughout my creative career I've always maintained and set big goals, big vision, and big action. What I was missing was alignment with those dreams and desires, alignment with why I so badly wanted to achieve them. That's what we'll cover in this next section on vision and goal setting. It will give you the tools you need to align your biggest dreams with the person you are, the person you want to be, and your deepest desires and needs. That, combined with the mindset you build and the faith you defined in section one, will make success inevitable.

CHAPTER 6

You Need a Vision for the Future of Your Business

Your vision guides your actions, and your actions create progress

We've done the work to begin mastering our mindset. We've explored the relationship between belief and action. We've embraced faith (not a passive belief, but an active process) as a means of creating success. That's a great start. But your business will struggle to succeed long-term without a vision to guide it.

As we transition from our foundation (mindset) into practical action (how to make money work for you, how to market, how to create no-brainer offers, etc.) we need to take some time to define the vision we're working towards, our purpose or reason that vision matters, and to outline our series of goals—the steps and accomplishments that will build on each other and help carry you from a five-figure creator to a six-figure business owner.

Again and again creatives tell me that they don't know how to keep going when their businesses feel small, futile, insignificant, or trapped in constant cycles of struggle, versus success and growth.

The dark times and growing pains in any business are hard to weather. Sometimes I think creatives feel this struggle particularly hard, because their businesses are such extensions of their creative selves. You're not just watching a retail idea you've come up with struggle; you're watching your identity struggle. Without the early signs of success—a big email list, lots of responses to their content, an ambitious new client—it becomes a struggle to stay motivated.

Often this doubt leads to a second, more existential question: "how do I deal with the tension of not wanting to do my work for money, but simultaneously needing money to survive?"

Vision is the answer to both of these frustrations.

First, let's define vision. In Beyond Entrepreneurship 2.0, Jim Collins writes: "Vision is what you put in place that encompasses your beliefs & values, your purpose, and your mission."

Depending on who you're listening to, the terms vision, purpose, and mission can start to blend, but we want to clarify how they are different.

Your vision is the grand, overarching plan that you have for yourself and your business. What you want it to become, who you want it to serve. Your vision will rarely change, which is why it is so important to come up with one at the beginning rather than letting one be decided for you (or avoided altogether).

Your purpose is the reason that you care about realizing your vision. Your purpose may slightly change the further you get into your business and as your audience's needs grow and evolve.

And your mission is your current plan on how to get there. Your mission may change regularly, every year or so, shifting as your business grows, adapts, meets, and then exceeds your initial vision.

Beyond that, you have strategies and tactics that aren't part of your vision but support the attainment of it.

Most businesses focus on strategies and tactics, and that's why they end up failing in the long term. Anyone who built their business on Facebook years ago had a rude awakening when the platform decided to start charging creators to reach their audience. That strategy was faulty, and unsustainable because it wasn't fully in their control. Those who survived, however, did so because they had a greater vision, and were able to adjust their strategy accordingly when that change occurred.

Your vision should empower you, motivate you, and pull you out of bed each day because of how exciting it is. It will galvanize your efforts, help make meaning in your life, and inform the work you do for the time that you're working on your business.

Once you have a vision in place, everything becomes easier. You now have a new context around the work that you're doing. While the frustrations of one day may render the work seemingly insignificant or unimpactful, your vision is what will remind you of your greater purpose and the long-term outcome you're working on. It will contextualize and minimize those bumps in the road we all face.

With that definition in place, it's easy to see the risk of not having a vision.

Without a vision, you risk going down a path that leads away from the future you want for yourself and your business. You could end up spending your time on projects that get you no closer to what you really want. At the end of them, these wayward projects you've chased after may, at best, feel like a wasted effort and a failure at worst.

How to Create a Vision for Your Business

You need to define a vision. Write it down and remind yourself every day what that vision is.

If you're taking this seriously—and I hope you are—carve out an hour or two in your calendar where you can be alone with your thoughts. In practice, what that looks like is imagining the dream future you want for yourself and your business. Get granular! Write down every detail you can think of. Here's what it looked like when I did this my first time.

I was at the 2019 Date With Destiny seminar that Tony Robbins puts on every year in Palm Beach, Florida. It was day four of the seminar, and we'd done a ton of work earlier in the week to understand our values, our desires, what motivates us, and what matters most. Taking all that mindset work into account, we got to step outside in the evening to write out our vision for the future. I have pages and pages of notes from that night—random words and phrases; big goals that I wanted to accomplish in the next year; and most importantly, what my next year was going to be about. I started looking ten years out—what kind of person did I want to become? What did I want to accomplish? Then I looked at five years out, then three, then two, then one. Each step closer came with more and more clarity. I knew, because I started at ten years out, that the things I wanted to do next year were in alignment with that vision. Every accomplishment next year would help me get closer to the person I wanted to become in ten years and would be in alignment with my greater vision. Since writing down my vision for the future that night, I have read it every morning and night, making it a constant refrain in my life. It's your turn to write down your vision. Get into a good mindset for this process. Turn off distractions. Close the door. And don't let yourself be interrupted.

Then, start writing. Here are some prompts to get you started:

- What do you really want?
- Who do you want to serve?
- What do you want to be spending your time doing each day?
- How much money do you want to make?
- How big is your business?
- How much money do you make?

Write these answers and thoughts in the present tense, as if you've already achieved them. Instead of "I will make $100,000 a year," change it to, "My business pays me $100,000 per year . . . "

Write, write, write until you can't think of anything else. Don't worry about how feasible or realistic these dreams are. This is your vision for the future, and you have no idea how the future is going to play out. The only limitations here are the ones you put on yourself, so don't put any limitations on your dreams!

Once you've done that, go through and pull out the parts that really give you an emotional response. The ones that make you smile, get your heart racing, or give you new ideas and excitement. Write those into a new document that you can read every morning and night.

Out of my list of things I wrote down, I had a mixture of goals and vision:

- Buy a new car
- Buy back my and my wife's time
- Write another book
- Travel to New Zealand
- Produce a movie
- Own buildings in Provo to develop
- New custom home

Owner of a $10 million per year company

Help 100,000 creators build resilient, profitable businesses

All of these massive goals informed a vision I was creating for my life in the future. A few stood out as things I desperately wanted sooner than later. Produce a movie. Buy back my time. Invest in creators.

This process led to two things in the next fourteen months from writing them down. I left my gig producing the TV show—buying back my time. I was no longer tied to a location, to working with people I didn't want to work for, and to someone else owning my time. I had freedom, which was a big part of the vision I saw for myself for the future.

Then in the spring of 2021 I produced a movie. As I've mentioned, this was a goal I'd been working to achieve for more than twelve years. I truly believe that if I hadn't gone through this process of creating a vision of what I wanted my life to be like that It may not have happened.

What I've experienced from this exact process has been incredible.

This book came from that process. My mind knew that to realize the vision of helping 100,000 creators build more resilient, profitable businesses, I needed a vehicle to help with awareness and to get people to join me in the work.

I also clarified the type of film and TV producer I wanted to be, so that I am fulfilled in my creative work and can contribute to the industry and the people I get to work with.

The focus I gained from clarifying my vision has made it easier for me to say no to other jobs doing things that don't align with what I want. I've since been able to increase my prices because of how focused I've been.

Without that focus, that vision, I would have taken any job, which would have distracted me from the work I wanted to do. I also left a good-paying gig on the TV show I was working on because it didn't fit my vision any longer, which opened up space for me to work on Craftsman Creative and other film and TV projects.

Let's look at a few sample vision statements that many creatives share, and then see if we can improve them so that they are more clear and more motivating.

"I want to grow my fanbase" to "I am selling out five hundred-seat venues on a twenty-five-city tour in two years from now.

"I want bigger clients" to "I have ten clients that each hire me for one project per quarter at $3,500 per project. I have added new services that will raise that rate to $5,000 per project for new clients."

"I want to buy back my time" to "I have left my job to pursue my own business, after reaching $6,000 per month as a side-hustle."

When you put it in present tense it makes it more real, and when you add specificity around the timeline, the number (money or gigs or fans), and the reason that it matters, it triggers a deeper belief and inspires greater action.

Your Vision Informs Your Work Today

Let's return to the struggle of not knowing how to keep doing the work that seems insignificant today.

With a bigger vision, the work you do today doesn't have to perform. You don't need 1,000 views or tons of responses to the thing you create today because it's not meant to perform independently of the other work you're producing.

Your vision allows your work to compound because it's now part of a bigger picture. That blog post that you wrote a year ago becomes a chapter of a book that becomes the basis of a lesson in a course or a foundational part of your coaching and consulting practice. That one blog post that didn't get any comments or likes the day it was posted may one day be responsible for thousands of dollars of income.

A personal example where I experienced this same struggle to stay motivated with writing every day.

At the end of 2020, I started a "60-Day Project" with the goal of starting a new blog and adding 60 new posts in 60 days. (I know, what was I thinking?!) Despite starting a new blog and writing 30-plus posts in 2 months, I felt like I'd failed because I didn't write 60, and only had about 2,000 people visit the site in those two months.

I gave up too early and never returned to the project. I'll never know what could have come from it if I'd kept up the habit and continued writing, despite not hitting my goal of 60 posts in 60 days.

Now let's compare that project to this book project.

The goal is to write a book in public, which means 30+ chapters in 100 days, tweeting about it every day using the #tweet100 hashtag, and having it as an important part of a bigger vision.

I want to help 100,000 creators grow their businesses. Some will make their first $1 doing what they love, some will double their already successful business, but most will learn what it takes to go from a five-figure creator to a six-figure business owner.

How?

It looks like this (more in the chapter on value ladder):

Tweets > Blog > Email/Newsletter > Book > Community > Coaching > Consulting

The first HALF of that vision is free content, but it makes the stuff that makes money ($XX book, $XXX community, $X,XXX coaching, $XX,XXX consulting/producing) work.

Without the entry point of the free content, like this book that was originally written in public for free, it is much harder to sell the bigger ticket items that are a big part of the vision I have for this business.

The context gained from having a bigger vision has changed the dynamic of the work.

It's essentially the same as before, writing 1,000-2,000 words a day and publishing them on the internet, but what felt like a task before now feels like I'm being pulled out of bed each day with excitement to contribute to the incredible audience that's giving me their time and attention to read what I'm writing.

How could I not write every day?!

When expanded out over months and years, even if this book only leads to 100 new email subscribers, the content will inform the community, the coaching, and the consulting work I intend to do next year for the people that need it to reach their goals.

I'm not just writing every day for no reason. Rather, each post is a building block that I'm laying as part of the foundation for my future vision. A year from now you could have a business, or another failed project you gave up on too early. The only difference is the vision that is giving context to the work. Remember, success is 80 percent mindset and only 20 percent strategy and skills. Especially when the strategy is the same.

CHAPTER 7

90-Day Goals

Set goals that can be achieved in the next 90 days to increase your likelihood of achieving them

With your vision in hand, you can now focus on your purpose and your mission. Your purpose is your reason for wanting to achieve the vision you set for yourself and your business in the last chapter. Your mission is how you are going to achieve it.

Too often people get overwhelmed by goals because they're not framed in actionable time windows that help them feel real. "Write a new song" is a lot harder for a musician to act on than, "Write a new song in the next week and workshop it within two weeks." Putting a time container on a goal gives it added weight and helps us imagine it as a reality (much like writing your vision in present tense). Once you have a vision for your business, set goals every 90 days to maximize your creative output.

The internet is littered with different variations of a quote about over/underestimating what can be done in a day, or a year, or a decade.

**Here's what I believe—we overestimate what we can do in a year, and we
underestimate the power of having a very clear plan to achieve it,
so we end up underachieving compared to the goals we set for the
year.**

Read that again.

Have you ever set a New Year's resolution, only to forget about it after a month or two, then felt a sense of regret or disappointment when you revisited that same goal the next year?

I have. That feeling sucks. It leads to a terrible mindset, which is the wrong mindset to be setting goals with.

You're going to flip the script and stop setting goals every year. The annual goal-setting ritual will now be reserved to update your vision for yourself and your business.

Goals, from now on, are not just "nice to haves." They aren't dreams. They aren't unrealistic. You need to see them as the desired outcome with a clear plan of action supported by a driving purpose.

In December of 2019, I attended a week-long seminar in Florida where I deeply ingrained these beliefs and this process. Since then I've practiced this and have done more in two years than the previous ten.

Here are a few of the goals that I set for myself over different 90-day periods:

- Buy a new car to provide adventure and excitement for my family
- Create a new business (twice)
- Grow my email list to over 1,000 subscribers
- Grow my Twitter following to over 1,000 followers
- Grow my personal income to six figures a year
- Produce a movie
- Produce seasons of television
- Produce a television pilot
- Learn to play jazz piano
- Film over a dozen online courses
- Buy back my time

Accomplishing any one of those goals in a given year would be amazing, but to have all of them accomplished in the last two years, including dozens of smaller projects. like building marketing or lead gen systems for my business, launching an app on Product Hunt, and more, feels superhuman, especially when I think about how they were done using 90-day windows. (I'm not saying I'm superhuman . . . but I'm not not saying that . . .)

If you're reading this, I want you to become superhuman as well and get more done in the next 90 days than you have in the last year.

That comes from setting goals in the right way.

Let's begin.

What Do You Want to Accomplish in the Next 90 Days?

The process starts with a question. What do you want to accomplish this year that will ultimately help you get closer to realizing your vision from the last chapter?

(If you didn't write out your vision, please do that first, as your vision is the guiding star that will help you navigate to that ultimate destination using your goals.)

Get out your notebook or open a new doc on your laptop/phone/tablet, and write IN THE NEXT 90 DAYS I WILL . . . at the top.

Then, turn off distractions, turn on some music to get your creative juices flowing, get into an empowering mindset full of belief and potential and faith, and write down all of the things you could possibly want to do in the next 90 days.

Don't edit, don't overthink it, don't second guess yourself. Just write!

IN THE NEXT 90 DAYS, I WILL...

- Grow my email list by 3,000 people
- Finish writing this book
- Find and hire an editor
- Presell 100 copies of the book
- Launch the beta for the coaching/ membership program.
- Launch six more courses on craftsman creative
- Produce a short film
- Take a trip overseas with my wife
- Go on a 3-day backpacking trip
- Buy a new computer
- Partner with an ad agency for the courses
- Get 100 signups for Benchmark App

My goals for the next 90 days

Take as long as you need, but be thorough. Think outside of just your business—what goals do you have for your family, for your relationships, for your personal life?

Now, once you've done that, take a nice deep breath and ask, "is there anything else?"

You'll be surprised that there usually is. Write that down as well!

Now that you have an exhaustive list full of potential and opportunity, you may look at it and feel overwhelmed. Don't worry! This is not meant to be a to-do list.

The next step is to look over everything you wrote down and circle the top three that get you the most excited, that are most aligned with your vision, and that you feel will bring you the most joy and fulfillment.

Notice that I didn't say the goals that will bring you the most money. That may be what you ultimately choose, but remember that we are combining mission and purpose with these goals. We need to bring that in at this point to ensure that what we're working on day-to-day is in alignment with our bigger vision. Often that comes down to purpose.

Do that now—circle the top three that you want to accomplish.

With Big Enough Reasons You Can Accomplish Anything

With those three goals, you need to now write down the reasons why you must achieve these goals.

Not because I said so. Not because your boss wants you to. Not because "it would be nice if . . . "

Big, strong, driving reasons that will give you the energy and the motivation to achieve these goals no matter what.

Ever hear about **hysterical strength**? It's the technical term for what happens when a mom sees her child trapped under a car and then somehow musters enough strength to lift the car to free the child. Hysterical strength comes from having a big enough reason so that nothing can stand in your way. That's the kind of purpose and reasons you need to support achieving each of your goals.

Next to your three circled goals, or on another paper, write down your reasons for achieving them. Some helpful prompts:

- Who will you become when you achieve this goal?
- What will it mean?
- Who will it serve?
- What will you be able to do once you achieve it?
- How will it feel?

Please do that now, and please, for the love of Taylor Swift, do not skip this step. It can be the difference between you achieving everything on your list and looking back 90 days from now wondering why nothing got done.

Now, you have one more step, because a goal without a plan is just a dream.

Create a Plan for Each of Your Top Three Goals

The last step is to systematically work backward from the goals that you want to achieve in the next 90 days and create a plan that informs the work you will do two months from now, one month from now, each week this month, and each day this week.

That's a lot. Here's what that looks like:

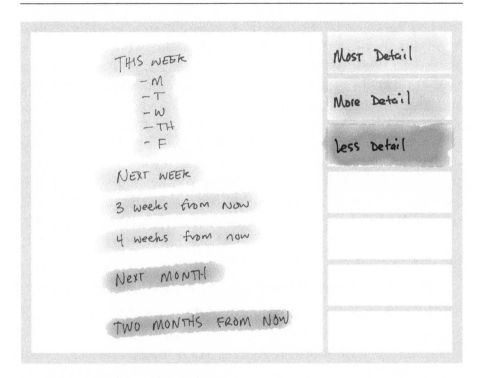

Your mission plan in detail

Start from the end and work backward.

In order to achieve your goal in the next 90 days, what needs to happen just before that? And just before that? And just before that? Keep asking that question of yourself and write down the answers.

For example, to finish writing this book, I need to:

- Implement the feedback from early readers into all chapters
- Finish writing all of the chapters
- Outline all of the chapters
- Finish the Table of Contents

This is vague, of course, but by thinking this way, looking back to see what needs to be done before you can move forward, the next steps become very clear. The first thing I need to do is to finish the table of contents. That could be done in an hour, and I can schedule that into my calendar for this week. Outlining all the chapters is a larger task. That will take much longer than a one-hour chunk of time, so I'll schedule in a few blocks this week as well to work on that. Writing all the chapters is a tougher task. Let's say I can write a draft of a chapter in one to two hours and that I'm writing about three chapters a week. Then I know writing another 24 chapters will take about 8 more weeks. I can now schedule those one- to two-hour writing chunks into my weeks, but not on specific days, because I don't know what my schedule will look like two months from now. Implementing the feedback is something I'll reserve for the last part of the third month. Now, I have a ton of clarity on what I'll be doing this week, and a somewhat clearer idea of what needs to happen in the next few weeks to stay on track.

Here's the secret: You need to revisit your plan every week.

This is not a one-and-done deal. Plans need to be adjusted and revisited every week in order to achieve your goals. Fill out a plan for each of your three goals. Then review the plan every week. I like to do that either on Sunday evening or first thing Monday morning, depending on what my schedule allows for.

Reread your goals, your reasons, and review your plan. What do you need to do this week to stay on track? Schedule those action items into your calendar for the week and make sure to show up! Little bits of progress every day, adjusting along the way, is how you achieve a goal through action.

This may be a new approach to setting and achieving goals for you. But it works, I promise; the highest achievers I know and look up to use a detailed process like this, which is optimized for achievement and progress.

Start this habit this week and review your goals every week, every month, and every three months—put the Manager in charge of scheduling this into your calendar. When you achieve your goals you can either add another and keep a rolling list of 90-day goals, or wait until the end of the 90-day period to start again.

CHAPTER 8

Take Massive Action Toward the Achievement of Your Goals

*Only by taking action will you
get where you want to go*

There's one last step to take now that you have your vision and your purpose and mission in place.

That step is to take action.

We could spend an entire book going into more and more detail on every aspect of the process, from honing your vision to discovering the deep purpose that's inside you, better aligning your mission and your goals to that purpose, and on and on.

But none of that matters if you don't take action!

So you take your vision, and your plan, and your goals, and you do something with faith that it will work out.

Commit to a Two-Week Sprint

With any new project or business, it takes for it to become a reality.

But that's not always what we want! We want instant results from our efforts. But spending a little time one day, then taking a few days off, then a little more time here and there, then another day off, creates zero momentum and nearly zero results.

There's a better way for those who desperately want to realize actual results quickly and efficiently.

Start with a sprint.

Wait. What's a sprint? I'm glad you asked. A sprint is a short period of time that you give everything you have to the mission or goal at hand. That means getting up early, staying up late, working during your lunch break and your commute, every waking hour that you can spare goes into this project. But, again, for a short period of time.

The intention is to create some momentum around your work that can continue once you let off the gas. The amount of momentum required is different for every project, but the more you do this process the better you'll get at recognizing when you have hit that point.

It feels like when you're riding a bike and you're pedaling as hard as you can, but then the road starts to slope downward, and the speed of the bike is greater than your ability to keep up your pedaling speed. More effort at that point doesn't make you go any faster. In fact, you can slow your pace to a nice easy pedal and still move forward. That's what we're creating by doing a sprint at the beginning.

Most people take the opposite approach when embarking on a new project or goal. They spend a few minutes here, a few minutes there, and never build any momentum because it's like hopping off the bike and expecting it to keep moving on its own.

Your project or business deserves more effort than that, so that's what we're going to do with this sprint.

Preparing for a Sprint

Just as you need to learn a bit about riding a bicycle before you take off at full speed, you need to do the same for your business.

Look at your goals and your plan from the last chapter. Now look at them while remembering that a sprint is about condensing four to six weeks of work into two.

That requires planning.

In order to sprint, you can't be thinking about how to shift gears, which lever is the brake, or how to balance on the bike.

You must have all of that already in place. For your two-week sprint, you need to have a very clear plan so you can focus 100 percent on execution.

Let's take the goal of growing an online community on a social network like Twitter. There are dozens (hundreds?) of courses you can take about how to grow your following on Twitter. I know, I've taken about five of them . . . Yet, none of them moved the needle!

Were they lying to me? Giving me bad suggestions? Did I just suck so badly that no one wanted to follow me?

No!

I approached it as a lazy stroll in the park. A little here, a little there, take a week off to focus on something else. It wasn't until I committed to a two-week sprint that the results finally happened.

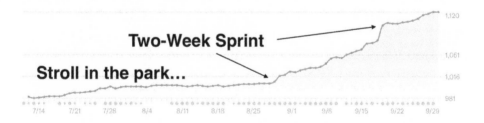

My Twitter following over 30 days

What that sprint looked like was informed by my plan, so that's what you're going to do now by asking this one simple question: What one action, done consistently over the next two weeks, will help me build momentum and achieve my goals?

That's it.

For me and my Twitter growth, it was scheduling tweets so that I was posting at least five times per day and commenting on ten to twenty other tweets every day on accounts that were bigger than mine.

That's. It.

Before, I would randomly tweet here and there, take a day off, and had no plan.

A plan + massive action = momentum.

So, choose one of your goals from the last chapter, and ask yourself what action, or actions, done consistently over the next two weeks will help you get the momentum you need to achieve the goal.

Important note—don't sprint on more than one goal at a time! Choose just one and do a sprint on that goal. You'll want to take two to four weeks off from that one before moving to the next, to ensure that the momentum stays and you're able to achieve the goal.

Bigger goals, ones that will take more than 90 days to achieve, will use the same approach, but instead of going from sixty miles per hour down to five miles per hour, you'll only back off the gas a little, to thirty-five to forty-five miles per hour. That way you don't lose momentum but can work at a sustainable pace without burning out. Notice you never go "into the red" and push to one hundred miles per hour. That's a recipe for burnout, which you want to avoid. (Yes, I realize I switched from a biking metaphor to a driving metaphor, but hopefully you're still with me.)

Open up your calendar, and schedule time every day for the next two weeks to work on your sprint for at least one to two hours per day. That can be an hour in the morning and an hour at night, or a two-hour block of time during the day, but schedule it now. Again, this is about taking action, not just having ideas and even plans. A plan without action is just a dream. And dreams don't pay the bills.

If you're working on writing a book, then you need to write for one to two hours a day during the sprint.

If your goal is to book more clients, then you need to set aside one to two hours a day to find new leads and reach out.

If you want to start a new community online then you need to dedicate one to two hours a day to inviting people to the community, engaging people there, and growing it to a point where it's more self-sustaining.

Being "prolific" isn't some God-given talent or blessing. It's about showing up every day and doing the work. This is what it takes. This is what professional creators do to succeed and reach their goals. You're going to be prolific for the next two weeks and take massive action toward the achievement of your goals.

And at the end, if you do the work and take massive action, you'll have proven to yourself that you can do this, that you're capable, that what you're creating is possible. You'll know that you have so much to contribute to the world and the people you seek to serve.

PART 3

Financial Mastery

*"When money realizes that it is in good hands,
it wants to stay and multiply in those hands."*

— Idowu Koyenikan,
Wealth for All: Living a Life of
Success at the Edge of Your Ability

Financial mastery is one of those things I wish I had learned much earlier in my career. I spent more than a decade working paycheck to paycheck, never having any savings, and never having any money to cover my butt in case of emergencies. And emergencies always come–a broken car that won't start; a last-minute flight home because a parent is in the hospital; covering the gap when payroll is due, and your client is now 120 days late on their invoice and you have no way to get that money sooner than they want to pay it.

I made a slew of terrible decisions over the years, mostly involving debt. I would turn to credit cards for those personal and family emergencies. I looked to gap financing and factoring to cover late invoices from clients, which ate up all of our profits and left us both short and in debt. When I left my video production business in 2017, I had taken on $15,000 in debt, personally, to keep the business afloat. It took more than three years to completely pay it all off.

Understanding the principles in this section on financial mastery will save you years of frustration, stress, doubt, and despair. When you build your business in this new way, you'll avoid debt; won't need to rely on investors or financing; and will have money in the bank set aside to pay your taxes, invest in your business, and pay you dividends as the business owner. It's a completely different approach than the one I used for the first two-thirds of my career, and I'm grateful that I've been able to learn and apply these principles and frameworks over the last few years. They saved us as we faced the uncertainty of COVID in 2020 and 2021. They helped us make more money than ever, start new businesses, and take advantage of new opportunities when much of the world was focused on fear and uncertainty.

What I want for you is a resilient, profitable creative business that supports the work that you do, so that you can do that creative work for many years to come. These financial principles are the foundation upon which you can build that business.

CHAPTER 9

Create a Minimum Viable Business

The way your business is structured may be the exact thing preventing its growth

It's time to dive in and build our six-figure business. We start with: Finances! I can hear your excitement from all the way over in Provo, Utah, where I live!

The reason we start here is that without a firm financial structure in place, everything else that follows may succeed in the short term, but not long term. Just as a house needs a solid foundation, we have our mindset. Then we add the framing—the structure—which is our business' finances. Then we'll add everything else—marketing, audience building, sales, and systems.

Let's start with understanding the Minimum Viable Business and how you can create one instantly just by understanding some key metrics and numbers. Remember, every business needs a Manager at times, and you're going to step into that Manager persona for this and many of the upcoming chapters.

Yay! Numbers!

Defining a Minimum Viable Business

Here's how I want you to look at your business:

What is the smallest amount of customers, projects, and revenue that you need for the business to be viable?

Knowing this number allows you to know when you have a viable business. That's the starting point you need to reach.

Then, using the following chapters in the book, you can learn how to grow the business from there.

You might be asking why this number matters. It's a matter of valuing your time. You don't want to grow a business that isn't viable. That would be like making more lasagna with spoiled ground beef. More isn't better; more is objectively worse. But if your business is viable, then it's ready for growth and worthy of your time.

The Ingredients of a Minimum Viable Business

Every business needs these three things:

1. A customer or client
2. A product or service
3. An offer that produces revenue

That's it.

Some businesses have a single customer or client. That single client purchases enough of the product or service to generate revenue that covers the cost of doing business, making the business viable. Other businesses operate by selling to many customers once or very infrequently. They may have lower-priced products, but are still able to sell enough volume to reach the revenue they need to make the business viable.

On the other hand, when one of the three above items is lacking, the business becomes unviable. (Yes, unviable is a word. I looked it up.) Without enough customers, a business can't survive. Without a valuable product or service, the business can't convince customers to buy. Without an offer that generates enough revenue, the business will fail, no matter how good its product or strong its customer base is.

Step One – Determine How Much Your Business Needs to Make

In order to understand what your "MVB" looks like, we have to make a few assumptions. Let's assume you either have a product or service that you currently sell, or that you know what you want to sell to your customers and clients.

If you don't yet know what you want to sell, unfortunately that's outside of the scope of this book, but you can look at some of the other resources on **CraftsmanCreative.co** for more information and stay tuned for a future book on how to break out of your day job and create a business based around your creative skills.

Now, get out a clean note page or open a new document, because we're about to get busy with some numbers! (If you have resisted stepping into the Manager persona, do that now!)

You'll work backward from whatever your minimum viable income is for your business, and you'll determine that using this formula: Your Personal Income ÷ 0.6

Why 0.6? Because, generally speaking, you want to have at least 40 percent of your business income set aside for taxes (15 percent), profit (10 percent), and operating expenses (15 percent). If you know exactly how much you set aside for taxes, profit, and operating expenses, then you can use a different number. For now, it's a good starting point. Said another way, if your business makes $100,000 per year, it can pay you $60,000 per year. So, if you want to pay yourself $5,000 per month, then divide by 0.6 and you'll get $8,333, which is what you need to bring in each month in revenue.

Here are some other examples that you can pull from if you don't want to do the math:

PERSONAL INCOME	BUSINESS/YR	BUSINESS/mo
$50,000 / yr	$83,333	$6945
$60,000 / yr	$100,000	$8,333
$70,000 / yr	$116,666	$9,722
$75,000 / yr	$125,000	$10,417
$80,000 / yr	$133,333	$11,111
$100,000 / yr	$166,666	$13,889
$120,000 / yr	$200,000	$16,667
$4000 / mo	$80,000	$6,667
$5,000 / mo	$100,000	$8,333
$6,000 / mo	$120,000	$10,000
$7,000 / mo	$140,000	$11,667
$8,000 / mo	$160,000	$13,333
$9,000 / mo	$180,000	$15,000
$10,000 / mo	$200,000	$16,667

Minimum Viable Income Table

If you're shocked by this, good! I want you to understand how important and real these numbers are. While your exact situation may vary by a few hundred (or even a few thousand) dollars, this chart might reveal that you're tens of thousands of dollars off in the way you've been thinking about revenue.

Keep in mind that these numbers represent your business's net income or "real revenue." If you sell a service that costs you $100 to provide, and you sell it for $200, your "net income" or "real revenue" is $100. We aren't accounting for the cost of goods sold or the cost to provide the service in these numbers. A photographer who charges $1,000 for a wedding but has $300 in film development costs only has a net income of $700 per shoot. That's the number that you should be using when looking at your minimum viable income, not the total or "gross income" numbers.

If you don't start with the proper numbers, everything else gets messed up down the line. With your business, step one is determining how much you want or need to pay yourself and how much your business needs to make in order to pay yourself that amount. Keep in mind that if you have business partners or employees, you'll need to double or add to the initial number that you want to pay yourself to account for splitting revenue or paying salaries.

For example, in my previous business, a boutique video and commercial production company, my business partner and I were each 50 percent owners of the company, and paid ourselves the same amount each month out of the business.

Some months we would make $15,000 or even as high as $25,000. Others we would only make $6,000 to 8,000. If I was a solo business owner, I could realistically take 35 to 60 percent of that revenue as owner's pay, which would be enough even during the low months. But when you have to split that owner's pay in half with another partner (or two or three . . .), you need to make more for that owner's pay percentage to cover everyone.

Say we wanted to pay ourselves $5,000 per month. That means $10,000 per month in owners' pay if you have two owners. Maybe 50 percent of your revenue gets paid out to the owners each month—you'd need $20,000 in revenue just to cover that cost. Adding one or more partners to your business significantly impacts your minimum viable income number, so be aware of that as you go through this chapter.

With your minimum viable income number in hand for your business, you can move to step two!

Step Two – Determine Your Minimum Viable Sales Number

It's time to look closer at your business. What is it that you sell? Do you have a single product or many? A combination of products and services? Or one or the other? What we're after is a number—how much money does a typical customer spend when they buy from or hire you?

If you are a graphic designer who charges, on average, $2,500 per project, then your number is $2,500.

If you are a musician who gets $1,000 per day in the studio, $250 per live show, and $5 per album that you sell, then you have three numbers. You can either average them out ($418.33) or do this exercise for all three (recommended).

This number is known as your average order value or AOV. When you multiply that number by the average amount that you sell each month, that leads you to your gross revenue.

Those two numbers—your AOV per number of orders and your gross revenue—should be the same!

To figure this out, look at your business for the last three months. Add up every single project and every single sale of your product. Total the amount of money made from the projects or services and divide it by the number you sold. If you sold a total of $25,000 (your gross revenue) over ten projects, then your AOV number would be $2,500. If you sold 100 products for a total of $12,500, then your average would be $12.50.

Then we take one last step.

Take your AOV number ($2,500 or $12.50 in our examples) and divide it by your monthly minimum viable income number from step one. If you need to make $15,000 a month, and your AOV is $2,500, then your minimum viable sales number is six per month. Gross Revenue (monthly minimum viable income) ÷ AOV = Minimum Viable Sales Number ($15,000 ÷ $2,500 = 6).

Now you know with absolute clarity how many projects you need per month in order to have a minimum viable business. I emphasize viable because plenty of freelancers and contractors run their business just below that viable number. If they need six projects a month to be viable, they often only have three or four, and so they live paycheck to paycheck and fail to ever create a profitable business.

The reason is that their business isn't structured to deliver more than four projects a month.

Read that again.

If they need six projects to be viable, but only have the ability to produce and deliver four, then they'll never have a viable business. They're set up to fail from the start. To prevent this, you need to take the third step and create a minimum viable offer based on these numbers from step one and step two.

Step Three—Create a Minimum Viable Offer

Your offer leads to revenue for your business. It's the vehicle that brings in cash flow that provides the much-needed oxygen for your business to survive and thrive. Without a viable offer, you will struggle to get the sales you need to have a viable business.

How do you know when you have a minimum viable offer? When you make enough money per sale and sell enough of your offer to create a minimum viable business. Said differently, a minimum viable offer connects the pieces we've already uncovered in steps one and two and makes it all work.

Let's go back to our graphic designer example. Her current business sells graphic design services for an AOV of $2,500 and can do four projects per month. We found that $2,500 per project isn't a viable offer because it leaves her unable to meet her minimum viable business revenue number of $15,000 per month.

She has three options (that are also applicable to you if you're in the same situation):

1. Increase her price per project to $3,750 ($3,750 x 4 = $15,000)

2. Increase the number of projects she can do per month ($2,500 x 6 = $15,000)

3. Add more products or services to her business

Depending on her situation, options one and two may not be feasible right now, and she needs a quick change to make her business viable as soon as possible. She could, in theory, take a few days to create a product that she could make $5,000/month selling, like an ebook, an online course, or stock graphics. Or she could create a smaller, $1,000-service package that can be done in one day instead of five, making more per hour and adding to her total revenue. These are just two ways you can evolve a business to reach your numbers (and ways that we'll look at in more depth later in the book). The goal is to get to a minimum viable offer for the products and services your business sells.

If you've ever felt stuck in your business, do the work in this chapter to build a framework for success and growth. Step into that Manager persona and let them run your business for a minute. It's the best way to gain clarity on what's really going on and identify the one thing you need to work on right now.

Ask yourself: what do I need to do right now to create a minimum viable business? Do you know how much your business needs to make? Do you have a minimum viable sales number? (If you do, are you selling the minimum amount every month to meet it? (More on that in the marketing and sales sections.) Do you have a minimum viable offer that will allow your MVB to work?

If you answered no to any of those questions, then tackle them one by one. Do the work and get clear on the current state of your business, as well as what you need to do to take it to the next level. That's your new mission for the next 90 days: determining what your new business needs to look like to be viable according to the criteria we just learned. You can add it to your mission from part one, or to your goals for when you purchased this.

The reason that artists get stuck making $30,000 to $80,000 per year is that they never step into the Manager or Entrepreneur persona and look at their business from a different perspective. Doing this may be hard, but it's a proven process that will help you bridge the gap from a five-figure creator to a six-figure business owner.

CHAPTER 10

Take Your Profit First

*Take profit first in your business
or risk having none at all*

With your new, viable business in hand, let's talk about one very important principle that leads to success:

Build a profitable business from the start and take your profit first.

Creators, generally speaking, aren't building businesses with the intent to scale like a rocket ship, have an exit, or build a unicorn. Those ideas are plentiful in the world of venture-backed startups, but our goal in this book is to build a resilient, profitable business that supports your creative work for as long as you want it to.

Perhaps someday you will consider selling your business, but that's not the norm. Your business is you. It's your work. So we're here to focus on how to make it resilient, and profitable. Resilient means it's built on a sound foundation and framework. Profitable means that it generates a profit with each sale of a product or service.

We discussed part of that in the last chapter on building a viable business. Now we need to take it one step further and begin to look at how you use the money that your business makes.

What Happens With the Money Your Business Makes

When you make a sale or a client pays an invoice, money enters your bank account. Let's say you just made $1,000. What should you do with that money?

You have a few options:

- Spend it
- Save it
- Invest it

In order for your business to function, you have some basic operating expenses, things like rent, internet, software subscriptions, and the tools you need to create your work or provide your service—a computer, phone, tablet, camera, art supplies, musical instruments, etc. If you don't set aside some money for those expenses, your business won't function properly and you'll find yourself going into debt or not having the tools you need.

You also need to pay yourself, so a percentage of that $1,000 should be set aside for that purpose as well. You've got taxes that will need to be paid in the future, so set aside some money for that. And once that's all done, whatever is left is considered profit! Right?

Well, that's how most businesses think about money. Profit is often defined as "whatever is left after expenses," and expressed like this: revenue – expenses = profit

The problem is that it's easy to let expenses grow to the point that they eat up all of the potential profit. Without profit your business isn't able to grow. There's no money to invest in new opportunities, new tools, or new projects, so the business reaches a certain level of revenue and expenses and stays there for years and years and years.

The only reason I was able to start Craftsman Creative—at the start of the pandemic and after being furloughed from the TV show I was producing, mind you—is that I had been setting aside a percentage of my business income in a separate profit account for over two years.

That money had accrued to thousands of dollars that I was able to use to pay my bills, but also invest in building a new business. Without that profit, this business wouldn't exist, and I may have had a hard time providing for my family and my lifestyle throughout the uncertainty of the last year.

Here's what you need to do: take your profit first, before you pay expenses or set aside money to cover taxes.

How To Take Profit First

Years ago, Mike Michalowicz wrote a book called **Profit First** that completely shifted the way I think about money in my businesses. It's what led to that business-saving profit account I mentioned above. And I highly recommend that you check it out.

In his book, Mike helps business owners think about profit in a different way by changing the order of how money that comes into the business is used. Instead of revenue - expenses = profit, it becomes: revenue - profit = expenses

This slight shift makes a world of difference. It guarantees that money is set aside to grow and invest in the business and provides quarterly distributions (think "bonuses") to the business owner. With my quarterly distributions, I've bought a watch, Air-Pods, a new phone, and plenty of other things that I wouldn't have thought of with my old mindset because I would have spent that money elsewhere in the business.

Remember, expenses will eat up as much money as you feed them, which is why you need to set aside profit first.

Here's how to do it: Start with 1 percent of your revenue. For every $100 that comes into your business, set aside $1 and put it into a profit account that is separate from your main business expense account. (Many banks will allow you to open multiple accounts under one login, and I'd recommend that you do this for your business as well.) Then, every quarter, add 1 percent, so that a year from now you're saving 4 to 5 percent of your revenue, and closer to 8 to 10 percent in two years.

That means that if your business makes $100,000, you're setting aside $10,000 to have money in the bank in case times get tough (resilience), and to pay out money to you as the business owner for building a profitable business.

Mike recommends that you do a "profit first session" twice a month, where you add up all of the revenue you made in the previous fifteen or sixteen days, then distribute that money out to the different areas of your business.

A typical budget for a creative small business may look something like this:

- Profit: 5 percent
- Owner's Pay: 60 percent
- Taxes: 15 percent
- Operating Expenses: 20 percent

Putting operating expenses last in the payout means that you have a set amount left over that you can spend on expenses, rather than having your expenses eat up all of the money first, leaving nothing left for profit, you to pay yourself with, or for taxes.

The above budget is a good one to work toward but going from 0 percent profit margin—because you've never considered it before—to 5 percent instantly is a huge jump. So, start with 1 percent for the next one to three months. It will get you into the habit of regularly (twice a month) setting money aside.

Then at the start of the next quarter (generally January, April, July, and October) bump that profit percentage up by 1 percent. You can do more if you feel comfortable, but this is a good pace to set to get to that 5 percent profit budget in the next year or so.

CHAPTER 11

How Much to Charge for Your Work

Charge enough to have a profitable business from the start

Too many businesses price their products and services arbitrarily or based on the "industry standard" or based on their experience. Those two may provide good starting points, but if you don't take it one step further, you'll price yourself out of business.

You need to understand your numbers and your business well enough to know what you need to charge in order to be profitable . . . from the start. Notice I didn't say "profitable once you reach a certain point." I mean profitable from the start, with every single sale and every single purchase.

Profitable from the Start

It's unlikely that you'll come out of the gate making $10,000 a month in revenue, unless you've built up enough demand prior to starting your business. That's entirely possible, but it's not the most common way that creatives start their businesses. (Important note—audience first, which we'll talk about in a later chapter, is a massive lever that can be used to start very profitable businesses.)

Instead, most creatives start out with a side-hustle. Maybe they're a graphic designer who starts taking some freelance projects in the evenings and weekends. Or they are someone with a 9-5 job in a non-creative industry who starts writing, or playing gigs, or taking photoshoots when they're not working.

The income from this part-time or side-hustle work isn't enough to leave their job, yet. If they don't follow this principle of pursuing profitability from the start, though, they'll never be able to make that jump from a 9-5 employee to a six-figure business owner.

Profitable from the start means that the income from every single project and sale follows the profit-first budget split covered in the last chapter.

- 5 percent profit
- 60 percent owner's pay
- 15 percent taxes
- 20 percent operating expenses

That means that you as the business owner don't take 100 percent of the money from your business and spend it. Instead, you set aside money for profit, taxes, and operating expenses. You might even set aside a greater percentage for profit than outlined here if your 9-5 is covering your income. The more money you save and invest in the business the more it will grow to become something you can do full time.

This is where a lot of creatives get stuck: They price their services without accounting for expenses, taxes, and profit.

I know a lot of photographers who would love to shoot film, but "can't" because of the cost. If they took their "digital" photography rate and cut and pasted it onto their "film" rate, they'd lose money on each shoot because they don't account for the extra expense of purchasing and developing film as well as the upkeep of their older cameras (operating expenses). Their business wouldn't be able to grow. In fact, if they started that business under that pricing structure, it would be doomed to fail.

Beyond just expenses, when creatives don't account for profit and taxes in their pricing, they inherently stunt their growth because there's never any money to invest in the business. In order for your part-time side hustle to lead to a full-time business, you have to price these things in from the start.

Reverse Engineer Your Pricing

There are two ways to look at how to price your work:

1. How much do you need to make?

2. How much do you want to make?

We'll start with number one and then look at number two as an alternative.

How much do you need to make? You can take the number you got from the chapter on building your minimum viable business and then divide that per month, per week, per day, per sale, or per project. You work backward from that outcome to get your pricing.

Let's do a service/project example and a product example.

PRICING YOUR PRODUCT OR SERVICE.

Say that you know that you need to make $4,000 a month to provide for yourself and your family. You look over the last three months of your business and realize you do, on average, four projects per month. At this point, you know you need to charge $1,000 per month, but that only covers your owner's compensation!

You then need to use the formula of $1,000 ÷ 60 percent to get the real price of $1,667 per project. Charge less than this and you run the risk of not having enough profit or enough money for taxes or operating expenses. Since $1,667 is a random-looking number, you could round up to $1,750 or even $2,000, creating even more profitability.

PRICING A PRODUCT

Say you sell your art or your music at $15 a pop. Once you account for fees, you end up with $10 that shows up in your bank account. You look at the last three months of sales and realize that you're selling 100 each month on average. 100 * $10 = $1,000. This is eye-opening because you either need to charge $75 per sale (netting you $66.67) or sell 6.6 times as many each month. (Remember, $4,000 owners pay ÷ 60 percent = $6,667 needed in monthly revenue).

You have options, and we'll talk about increasing sales in a later section, but you realize that unless you charge more or sell more, you won't get to your minimum viable business with that pricing structure of $10 per album and only 100 sales.

How Much Do You *Want* to Make?

This is where most people spend their time, thinking about how much money they want to make, versus how much they actually make or how much they need to make. Want is the destination. Not the beginning. If you skip past figuring for need, you'll never get to this stage.

You have to understand the realities of pricing, expenses, and budgeting in your business if you want to be profitable from the start and grow. Ignoring these realities will leave you stuck exactly where you are.

That being said, it's fun to reverse-engineer how much you want to make. Say, again, you want to make $100,000 in personal pay from your business. That means that your business needs to make $100,000 ÷ 60 percent = $166,667.

Or $13,889 per month.

Or $3,205 per week.

Or $457 per day.

How do you reach that goal? Through the same combination of the number of projects or sales you can generate per month divided into those numbers. If you can do four projects per month, then divide $13,889 by four to get $3,472 per project. (But let's round up to $3,500 to make it a nice round number for the client.) If you currently charge $1,000 to $2,500 per project, you'll need to figure out if you're going to sell more projects per month or raise your prices.

The specifics around how to structure a deal to be more valuable—for both you and the client—are covered in the next chapter, but realize that you can increase your pricing at any time for any reason, the most important being that you can't stay in business if you don't make enough money. Every business should understand this principle, but it seems to escape creators. They often think, for a myriad of reasons, that they can't increase their prices and charge what they need to charge to have a viable business.

You can charge whatever you want! (Getting people to pay for it is a subject for a later chapter). But you need to get over the idea that you can only charge $X per hour, or per project, or per day, or per item.

It's all arbitrary. There are people who charge $79 for an ebook. $10,000 per wedding for photography. $250 an hour for design work. You can, too, even if you're just starting out or have less experience than someone charging half that.

Raising your prices to the level you want, versus need, or feel you deserve, all goes back to the chapters on mindset. If you believe that you aren't worth more than $40 an hour, you won't ever charge more than $40 an hour. This kind of thinking is much more damning to your business than anything you'll ever do (or not do) regarding sales or marketing or pricing. It prevents you from realizing your actual worth, which prevents you from ever growing.

The minute you start increasing your self-worth, the minute increasing your pricing becomes not just possible, but essential. You have to believe that you are worth more and that you can provide more value than anyone else around you.

That, and how to structure a deal properly, is what we'll cover in the next chapter.

CHAPTER 12

Structure Deals Properly

Understanding the different ways that deals can be structured can increase revenue for your business

In this chapter, we'll discuss a few ways to structure deals in your business so that you can ensure profitability from the start. Again, that is your goal. You want every possible deal to be profitable. As you'll learn in this chapter, there are many ways to make that happen.

Understanding the various ways to structure deals will help you gain financial mastery over your business. It will help you become more profitable, more confident in the way you run your business, and more resilient so that your business can exist for much longer.

Let's dive in!

Typical Deal Structure

This chapter is very much geared toward projects and services, and less about selling products. However, after understanding the sales ladder (explained in the sales section) you will know that every business should have both products and services, so don't skip this chapter because you think it's not for you. In short, the sales ladder approach means that you have a number of different product and service offers at multiple price points, ranging from $X and $XX, all the way to $XX,XXX.

Most freelancers, when structuring the deal for their services, will simply estimate how much time they expect the project to take, and multiply that by their current hourly rate. So a ten-hour project at $50 per hour is a $500 project.

While this structure's simplicity is helpful, it leaves a lot on the table, and doing projects like this over and over makes it harder to make room for the bigger projects that will grow your business.

There are only so many hours in a week. Even if you are willing to work fifty hours a week, and can get five client projects booked every week, you'd have a hard ceiling at $2,500 per week (5 projects x $500 = $2,500). While you may be happy making $10,000 or so per month, most creators aren't booking that much work, or would burn out trying to deliver that many projects per week.

There are many more ways to structure a deal to maximize profitability and therefore grow your business—remember that the point of taking profit first is to save it for growing your business. In **The Art of Profitability**, Adrian Slywotzky outlines more than twenty different deal structures, or "ways to get paid," that are different from the typical "time for dollars" structure mentioned above.

I want to offer two here that will expand your perspective and help you take the next step toward financial mastery.

Profit-Based Deal Structure

The structure looks like this—Imagine a video ad agency that gets $XXX,XXX for the cost of creating and producing a video for a client, as well as purchasing the first X months of video ads on Facebook and other platforms. But, in addition, they also get a percentage of sales that occur from their ads.

This one is fairly straightforward and can be used in conjunction with the standard "time for dollars" model, or as a replacement. Whether you use it together or instead depends on your level of trust with the client who is hiring you.

Services businesses can thrive using a profit-based structure because it allows you to participate in the upside, position yourself as a partner, not a vendor, and grow your business substantially.

The first time I saw this model was with the Harmon Brothers, a commercial video company based in Provo Utah. They make viral video ads for companies and have helped their clients grow exponentially by controlling the ad campaigns on social media platforms.

This hybrid model—not fully "time for dollars," not fully profit-based—allowed them to cover their costs as well as participate in the upside, and grow to an eight-figure-a-year business in record time.

I've personally gone to the extreme end of this model with Craftsman Creative. I pay out of pocket for the production costs for every new course on the site. The course partner brings their audience and helps market and sell the course online. We split the backend profits 50/50, so there is complete alignment, and I only get paid if the courses sell and make money.

Here are the behind-the-scenes numbers on just one of the courses. If I had done the vendor/time-for-dollars model, I probably would have charged $3,000 to $5,000 for a course. That includes no profit margin and no upside but would cover my time ($1,000 per day for three to five days of work). That model has a hard ceiling of $5,000.

But, because I structured the deal differently from the start, that single course partner has done more than $25,000 in sales in eighteen months. With that 50/50 split, I've made $12,500—two to four times more than what I would have made using the "standard" model.

Yes, I took on more risk upfront, and yes, it took longer to make that $12,500 than it would have taken to make the $3,000 to $5,000 upfront. But the upside is undeniable and continues today! I'll earn 50 percent of each course sale as long as it's on my site.

Here's how to implement this with your clients:

1. Know your worth.

2. Understand the potential upside

3. Cover the downside to trade for upside

Know Your Worth

Understand how much value you are creating for your client. How many hours are your services saving them? How much is there time worth per hour? How much expense are they saving by out-sourcing through you, versus doing it in house? Understanding these points before you put a deal together will show a client that you know their business and understand what you're bringing to the table.

Understand the Potential Upside

This requires that you spend some time thinking about the way(s) your services will help your client make money. Is your design going on their website? Will it be part of a marketing campaign? Is your video for their YouTube channel, or will it be the hero video on their homepage? How will your photos be used?

If your client is using the assets you create for them to sell products, there is potentially a lot of upside, which you can participate in if you understand what's possible.

I made videos for a realtor at one point at $500 a pop, because I figured it would take about five hours of my time between filming and editing. But, at one point, I realized that 6 percent of a $1,000,000 home is $60,000 (give or take), and that I was charging less than 1 percent of the realtor's income from that sale. Had I structured it differently, I could have asked for a percentage of the realtor's revenue, rather than a flat, hourly fee.

Cover the Downside to Trade for Upside

In certain situations, there are projects that require money up-front to cover costs. Video production is one of these—in order to produce a commercial, there are costs for labor, equipment, locations, food, insurance, and more. Most video production companies ask the client to cover these costs by paying part of their budget up-front, sometimes as much as 50 percent.

What you could do instead is cover the production cost yourself and ask for a percentage of sales or equity in the company. Sandwich Video famously structured their deals this way. They would cover the production costs in exchange for equity in the companies they were producing videos for, companies like Slack, Warby Parker, Casper, Square, TikTok, and more.

Imagine the upside of owning parts of these billion-dollar companies. You can do the same—if on a smaller scale—by understanding your worth, the potential upside, and covering some of the downside to trade for upside.

Value-Based Deal Structure

It's time to stop positioning yourself as a vendor and start positioning yourself as a partner. This one crucial insight can be the key to huge success for service providers.

Vendors sell commodities, things that can be haggled on price and found from dozens (hundreds?) of other vendors. You don't want to be a vendor. You want to be a partner. Partners bring more than just services to the table. They themselves are a valuable asset to be working with. Partners don't haggle on price. They understand the terms of the deal and find a fair structure that works for everyone involved. Everyone brings what they need to the table, and everyone participates in the upside.

For Craftsman Creative, I bring my fifteen-plus years of film and TV production to the table, as well as cover all the cost for production and editing, web design, marketing, and advertising, as well as proven frameworks for launching and selling courses.

The course partners I work with bring their talent, their experience, their content, and their audience. The deal is structured as a 50/50 split on sales, 50 to the partner, 50 to Craftsman Creative. Of that 50, 20 goes to ongoing ad spend, and 30 is revenue for the business. This perfect alignment stems from positioning myself and my company as a partner, not a vendor for hire. I've had people ask how much it would cost to hire me to produce a course for them, and I've turned them down. I'm not a vendor, so the only way to work with me is as a partner.

Think about how you can do this for your business. The thought exercise alone will open new doors, new structures, new ways of working with clients.

Who is your typical client? What do they need beyond just the creative output? Do they need help with the concept, the distribution, the monetization? What other experience do you have that could benefit them that differentiates you from the crowd of competitors in your market? Harmon Brothers combined commercial video production with ad buying and management. Craftsman Creative takes video course production and marries it with web design, ad management, product launch strategy, and affiliate support. What other things can you combine that makes you truly unique, and therefore more valuable as a partner than any other vendor?

The important thing to remember is that you want to ensure profitability from the start with your deals. You can work for free or at a loss for certain situations and clients in order to get more work in the future, but it's not a sustainable deal structure. Do it strategically, not because you don't value yourself enough to charge more and have a profit margin.

CHAPTER 13

Increase Your Profit Margin

*This simple framework will help you
immediately raise your prices*

There is just one thing you need to know from this chapter:

Raise your prices.

When I started freelancing in 2006, I set my prices based on what my competitors were charging, $35 an hour, and then I discounted that rate by $10. Yes, I charged $25 based on a bunch of things that had nothing to do with my business or the value I was creating for people, and I was charging for my time.

Basically, I did the opposite of everything we covered in the last chapter.

Ten years later my prices had risen to $100-plus per hour because I'd learned some of the lessons I'm teaching in this book, and because I was running a company, rather than charging as a vendor.

When you run a company, you have expenses—taxes, overhead, operating costs, and, yes, profit. While profit isn't an expense, it's still something that your business needs to make on every project and every sale whenever possible. Again, there are rare times that you'll discount your price or even work for free, but your standard pricing should allow for a decent profit margin that allows you to grow your business.

Yet, I still see too many creators operating like freelancers instead of business owners. As the subtitle of this book states, the secret to shifting into six-figure work is by going from a creator to a business owner. And a big part of that is charging like a business.

So, at the risk of sounding redundant, here, again is the most important insight from this section: Be profitable from the start. The way to do this is to raise your prices—the most important insight from this chapter.

If you are charging $25 an hour as a freelancer, you can instantly, today, raise your prices to $40 per hour. Because you're a business that pays you $25 an hour, therefore you need the other $15 to cover profit, taxes, and operating expenses.

Take the hourly rate (or monthly rate) that you want to pay yourself, and perform this equation to determine the hourly (or monthly) rate for your business: Your Pay ÷ 60 percent = New Rate

If you need to pay yourself $2,000 per project, then you need to charge your client $3,500. Not $2,000.

How to Charge More for Your Work

The immediate question that inevitably pops up when I talk about this is, "how?" "How do I charge more?"

Accomplishing this takes two tactics. First, you need to shift your mindset. Next, you need to shift your language around your services to raise your rates with your existing, as well as future, clients.

Shift Your Mindset

First, put an end to seeing yourself as a freelancer, and instead start to look at yourself as a business owner. You're a partner, not a vendor, remember? As a partner, you're covering some of the downside, or the risk, for the client, and you deserve to be paid more in return. Embody this new persona, put on the entrepreneur hat, and make the change. Once you've done that, here's how to raise prices with your current and future clients.

Raise Your Rates with Your Current Clients

With your current clients, you can send a simple email explaining the realities of the situation:

"Hello {client}!

I'm reaching out to let you know that I'm dedicating more time and resources to my creative business. This means that I'll be working with you more as a partner, rather than a vendor.

As you may expect, this comes with an increase in overhead, as well as taxes and investment in the business, which means that my rates are increasing.

Any current projects will remain at the same rate, but going forward my new rate will be [fill in the blank for your business].

This will allow me to serve you at a deeper level and provide even more value to the projects that we're working together on.

I'm excited for this progress and that I get to continue to serve you in this way. Thank you for the opportunity to serve you and your business!"

And for future clients, it's even easier: Raise your rates. That's it. Update your pricing page, quote the new rate in any estimates, and change your product pricing tags.

They don't have the context of what you used to charge, so you don't need to work about them thinking that you "raised" your rates. It's just "the rate."

But what if raising your rates makes you more expensive than your competitors? That's what we'll cover in the next section on marketing, which includes positioning, and the section after that on sales.

CHAPTER 14

Increase the Age of Your Money

Increasing the age of your money will help you grow your business and remove the financial stress of living paycheck to paycheck

All of the things I've talked about in this section on finance are geared towards getting your business off on the right, profitable foot, and to understanding how to grow it profitably after.

In the startup ecosystem, this is often referred to as "bootstrapping," where you rely on the money you make to grow your business, rather than try to raise money from outside investors.

You adopt the principles I've covered here that make sense for you, the ones that you feel tugging at you to give them more attention, or you can ignore them completely.

But one principle stands out as one of the simplest and most impactful: Increase the age of your money. This one idea incorporates so much of what this section covers, and it's a very clear, measurable metric.

I got this idea and phrasing from the fine people at YouNeed-ABudget.com, the app I've used to track my personal finances for years. In the top corner of their app, it shows you the "age of your money," which they define as the length of time your money has been in your bank account before you spent it.

44 days
Age of Money

If your money were only a few days old, then you'd be experiencing the paycheck-to-paycheck lifestyle. Money comes in one day and gets spent the next. Once you reach fourteen days, you have a little bit of breathing room, and thirty-plus days means that you're living on the income from last month.

That's the ideal scenario. Having enough "runway" means that you have the ability to pay your bills, cover your expenses, grow your business, and pay yourself what you want to be paid.

If there's one thing to actively do for the next three months is to focus on that singular goal—increase the age of your money. You can do this simultaneously with your earlier 90-day goal or make it your new 90-day goal after you've accomplished the others that you've set.

Here are three ways to do it:

- Save
- Cut your costs
- Add a new product or service revenue stream

Save to Increase the Age of Your Money

The simplest of the three is to simply save money for a little while.

Drive your car less. Wait to buy that new piece of equipment or rent out that office space. Skip a month of hiring contractors and do more of the work on your own.

Whatever it looks like for your business, you can try and save up thirty days of money over the next three months. If your monthly expenses are $4,000, then you need to save $1,333 each of the next three months. And if your money is already fourteen or fifteen days old, then you only need half that amount.

Cut Your Costs to Increase the Age of Your Money

The next step can be used simultaneously or on its own if saving isn't an option right now. Cutting costs means going through all your expenses and either cutting them out or cutting them down.

Cutting out means removing unnecessary expenses from your spending.

Look at:

- Subscriptions
- Apps with a monthly fee
- Eating out
- Buying equipment
- Upgrading equipment
- Contractors and freelancers

What can you cut out? What do you no longer need, even if it's just for a short period of time? What expenses can you combine to get more for less?

Cutting down means negotiating the costs or finding more cost-effective options.

- Pay annually for app subscriptions (often saving 20 percent or more)
- Negotiate project rates with your contractors, instead of hourly rates
- Bring your lunch instead of eating out every day

Go through your bank statements for the last three months to see everything that you've spent money on. Look at what you can realistically cut out or cut down to increase the age of your money.

Add More Revenue to Increase the Age of Your Money

This is easier said than done, yes, but finding long-term success is often as simple as increasing the amount of money coming into your business while keeping what's going out the same. For example, it's often easier to make an extra $1,000 per month through a new product or service offering than to cut $1,000 per month.

In the next chapter, we'll discuss how to invest in assets that compound over time and bring in new revenue for your business. The key takeaway from this chapter is that your "age of money" is an important metric to keep track of.

If you don't want to use YNAB (which is more of a personal finance tool anyway), you can simply look at how much money is in your bank account and compare that to your monthly expenses. If your monthly expenses are $12,000, then you spend roughly $400 per day. If you have $4,000 in your account, then the age of your money is ten days.

You can track this however you see fit, and we'll talk about other metrics to track and ways to do so in the section on systems and leverage, but for now, identify your current age of money and what you need to add to your bank account to get past the thirty-day age mark.

CHAPTER 15

Invest in Assets That Compound

Creating a collection of digital products that sell automatically is one of the best financial decisions you can make for your business

Writing this on the same day that Apple announced its new (insane, bonkers, extraordinary, unbelievable) line of MacBook Pro's seems . . . serendipitous?

So far in this section we've covered how to determine what a minimum viable business looks like for you, how to take profits first, how to determine how much to charge to ensure profitability, how to structure deals to consistently reach that amount and then grow, how to increase your profit margins, and the importance of tracking the age of your money to set yourself up for growth. Whew!

In this chapter, we'll talk about the last thing to consider on our way to financial mastery, where to invest your time and your money. Once you have a successful, profit-prioritizing business up and running, you can start better investing, directing, and spending those profits to ensure more growth. But where should we direct our money?

In short:

Invest in assets that compound over time.

Let's define what an asset is and then dive into why it will benefit you to have this framework for your business.

So, What *Is* an Asset?

Technically speaking, according to Investopedia.com, an asset can be defined this way: "An asset is a resource with economic value that an individual . . . owns or controls with the expectation that it will provide a future benefit . . . An asset can be thought of as something that, in the future, can generate cash flow, reduce expenses, or improve sales."

Important in that definition is the bit about providing future benefits. Assets can bring in cash flow, create efficiency, or improve the cost for a result. It's always interesting to me, however, how these definitions easily apply to a business that has products or manufactures things, but not to creative businesses that may be purely digital projects or services.

What would a photographer consider an asset? Well, their camera would easily apply as it allows them to create cash flow, right? The same could be said for their computer, which they use to edit the photos. Both are items that they, or the business, owns and that create "future benefit." A musician may consider their instrument(s) an asset. Possibly even their car that they use to travel to gigs and shows. What about that new lens? Or an upgraded computer? Or a new car? This is where it gets interesting to me, and why I want to focus less on physical assets for digital businesses, and more on digital assets that provide creators "a future benefit . . . "

Higher Level Assets – Things That Compound on Their Own

For the sake of this chapter, I want to focus on digital assets that can compound over time, meaning the more of them that you have, the more they work together to create even more "future benefit." Assets that you can own completely and that can be created once and sold an unlimited number of times without your direct involvement in each sale are the focus.

Some examples include:

• Stock photos that can be sold or licensed

- Music recordings that can be sold or streamed or licensed
- Books that can be sold to interested readers
- Online courses that students can enroll in
- A paid newsletter or community that anyone can subscribe to

These digital assets can be created in a way that allows them to be sold in an automated fashion—whether by you or by others. And the more that you make—whether by creating different asset types or more of the same asset type—the easier it is to make more and more revenue from those assets.

If an average stock photo makes you $10 per month, then one hundred could make you $1,000 a month, and one thousand could make you $10,000 per month. They compound because when someone discovers one of your photos, they may look at your entire profile and purchase more. This compounding only happens if you have many assets (stock photos in this case), opposed to just one or two.

Musicians with a deep library of albums can benefit from compounding as well. When someone discovers a song on a playlist from Spotify or Apple music, they click through to a musician's profile to listen to more music, which leads to more streams and purchases.

When I started Craftsman Creative, I wanted to put this framework to the ultimate test—by only creating assets that compound. I didn't offer any services. I didn't offer any physical products. Only digital assets that compound the more that I produced.

I started with two of my own courses. While they didn't produce much revenue when I launched them in April of 2020, they're now assets that I can link to in my email courses and newsletter. The more people that subscribe to those assets, the more that people discover my courses and purchase. They compound because of how well they work together in the business.

Since that time, we have produced more than a dozen other courses that all compliment each other—multiple hand-lettering courses, multiple photography courses, and multiple business courses. When someone purchases one, it's easy to tell them about the others that they might be interested in, and some people buy. All of this happens automatically without any direct involvement in each sale—tens of thousands of dollars per month with or without me.

When I was producing a movie for two months in April and May of 2021, I didn't spend any time on Craftsman Creative. (I don't recommend ignoring your business for two months, by the way.) But during those two months, this is what happened with course sales:

Month:	2/21	3/21	4/21	5/21	TOTAL
COURSE 1	$1,264	$305	$150	$425	$2,144
COURSE 2				$129	$129
COURSE 3	$562		$248	$495	$1,305
COURSE 4	$1,145	$1,020	$3,865	$1,169	$7,199
COURSE 5		$49			$49
COURSE 6				$1,729	$1,729
AVERAGE	$990	$344	$1,421	$789	—
TOTAL:	$2,971	$1,374	$4,263	$3,947	$12,555

The courses brought in more than $12,000 in the four months that I was working on the film, and more than $8,000 between April and May—the two months that I didn't touch Craftsman Creative. That's the power of owning assets that can compound over time and be sold in an automated fashion.

Crazy.

Again—I sold more in two months of not working on the business than in the previous two months where I was working on the business part-time. I'm doing everything I can to live this principle and share the results with others because I believe that it's the right next step for creators earning most of their revenue through projects and "time for dollars" work.

Musicians can go from just playing gigs to selling and licensing their music.

Photographers can sell their photos to their clients as well as license stock photos that bring in recurring revenue.

Writers can self-publish a book compiled from their best articles and essays on their blog. That's essentially what James Clear did to go from a niche author to a household name with his book *Atomic Habits*.

Designers can sell their work on Gumroad like **Tr.Af** did with his icon sets. He ended up making not just $5,264, but more than $25,000 in two days. That's a massive "future benefit" created by a single asset that still sells to this day.

The question for you, now, is "what assets are you going to create for your business?" Think about the digital thing that you can make and sell. Then think about how you can get it in front of your audience in an automated way.

You can use an email automation app like **ConvertKit** to deliver emails automatically to new subscribers. You can link to it in the bio of your emails or your **social media accounts**. You can set up a free store for your digital products (books, music, photos, art) using **Gumroad**.

Start small with something simple that you can charge $X for. Then add more, then use the Sales Ladder (covered in the section on Sales) to add $XX and $XXX assets in the same way. Start with a digital product like stock photos, an ebook, an EP with a few demo recordings of your songs. Then move up to an album, a short online course, a more thorough ebook, your own artwork. Then up another level into higher-priced products and services like coaching, mentoring, portfolio reviews, site audits, and hourly work. Your four- and five-figure products and services come later when you're a bit more established and have the demand from your audience for a larger "job to be done," which we'll talk about in the next section of the book.

How to Create Compounding Assets

It's important to create assets that compound and build off each other, not just a suite of disconnected products. Compounding occurs when you have either more of the same type of product or create complementary products.

The reason for this is two-fold:

- What happens when someone new discovers your work
- What happens when you announce something new to your existing audience

When someone new discovers your work, they may just buy a single product, but they will often click around your site to see what else you sell. If they enjoyed the first book, it's likely they'll enjoy your other books. If they liked one song, they'll likely enjoy all of your music. That discovery then helps people become fans who purchase more of your work. Then, if you've set it up properly with an email list or some other way to connect with and reach your audience, when you release something new, your existing fans are the most likely to buy it.

Tiny Little Businesses launches new products and courses every year, sometimes just updating an existing product with new information or structure. Most of their enrollments come from people who have previously purchased courses in the past or have been on their email list for some time—often years.

Holly Homer initially created a massive blog that shares activities for kids. She now regularly gets 10 million (yes, million) visitors a month to her site. She expanded that by offering complimentary products—books, a coaching business for others wanting to build an online business, and a bundle of online courses. Each of these products came from the demand of her audience. They told her what they wanted to learn from her, and she created products around those desires that now sell automatically because of how she's set up her business.

I encourage you to take the step to doing one of the best things you can do for your financial future by creating an asset that can compound over time. This isn't just for people making millions of dollars and who have millions of fans, either. Everyone starts at zero. You can start with a single product, even if you are just starting out on your creative journey.

Doing so allows you to escape the rat race of starting each month at zero and hoping to find enough projects and gigs to cover your expenses. Even an extra $100 means you're starting that much ahead each month. Then you add another and another, and things start to compound. You're then starting each month at $500, then $1,000, then multiple thousands of dollars.

Imagine your business making $10,000 to $20,000 per month just from these digital assets. What would that feel like? What would that free you up to do, to create, to experience? How would it change your life?

In order to get there, you have to start with one, then add another, then another. Then you optimize the process of selling these assets (which we'll cover in the last section on Systems and Leverage). This framework is one of the biggest things I wish I'd learned early in my creative career, and I'm excited to be able to share it with you in this book. Come up with a product that you can create in a day or two. Put it up using the links in this chapter. Then tell your audience about this new thing you've made, how it will make them feel, or how it will benefit them.

Start small, start now.

But you make it sound so easy! Yes, I hear you. Writing it out in a book is infinitely easier than putting it into practice in real life and getting the results that you want from that effort. Here's the thing—the simple act of focusing on these concepts is a step in the right direction. If you take a few minutes every day to build an asset that can compound, that you own completely, that you can create once and sell an unlimited amount of times thanks to the wonders of the internet, you're on the right path. That's all it is: taking steps in a new direction that could compound and grow over time.

If you only ever trade your time for dollars through gigs and one-off client projects, you'll never build a portfolio of assets that you own and that can pay you in the future. So start now, start small, and create your first asset. It could be as simple as a ten-page e-book that teaches your audience how to accomplish one simple goal, or gets them from A to B. "How to turn your notes into song lyrics," or "how to create digital hand lettering," or "how to increase your prices for your wedding photography packages."

Take a weekend, write it out, design it in something like Apple Pages or Canva, and then sell it using a site like ConvertKit or Gumroad. Just a few days from now you could have your first asset working for you and paying you while you sleep. So get started.

CHAPTER 16

A Portfolio of Small Bets

*The secret to not just becoming—but
staying—a professional creator.*

❖ ❖ ❖

In 2020, Daniel Vassallo blew up on Twitter going from ~12,000 to nearly 100,000 espousing his "portfolio of small bets" approach to crafting a lifestyle on his terms.

Daniel Vassallo @dvassallo · May 7, 2020   •••
Don't build a product.

Build a **portfolio of small bets**.

Once you adopt this perspective, it becomes a lot easier to figure out what you should be doing (and not doing).

💬 34   ⟲ 132   ♡ 1K   ⬆️

https://twitter.com/dvassallo/status/1258518741106618368?s=20

The idea is that rather than putting all your eggs in one basket—be it with a job/employer, one big client, or having any sort of "single point of failure"—you diversify and have more, smaller bets.

Justin, as he explains in the Twitter thread, started with consulting. Then he doubled his rates. Then he added a digital product, an online course to help people master LinkedIn. If any one client went away, he'd still be fine. Adding the product gave him an even more resilient portfolio.

All of this got me thinking about my own portfolio of small bets. Did I even have one? It turns out I did, and I realized something that blew my mind.

Here's my current portfolio of small bets, in descending order of cost:

- **Film/TV/Commercial Producing** ($30,000+ per project, $1,000+ per day)
- Owner of **Craftsman Creative** ($5,000/mo)
- Creative Business Consulting ($5,000/mo)
- Creative Business Coaching ($1,000/mo)
- Hourly Consulting Calls ($250/hour)
- Online Courses ($79-997)
- Co-founder of **Benchmark App**
- And, coming next year:
- Craftsman Creative Membership Community ($199/year)
- **Craftsman Creative Book** ($20+)

So, yeah, nine different "small bets" that I've built over my career, most of them over the last eighteen months.

Here's what blew my mind: I have already built a portfolio of nine small bets! I had no idea that I had so many. I think if you'd asked me off the top of my head, I would have said three or four.

There are two places where creatives get stuck.

The first is not creating a portfolio of small bets that can help them get the freedom they want through their creative work. The second is building too many at once and not giving each enough attention.

I have the second problem.

In total, this portfolio delivers a nice six-figure income for me and my family. But right now it's very imbalanced—one or two of them represent more than 90 percent of my income.

So my goal for 2022 is to balance out the portfolio. And my challenge is for you to take stock of your own creative business and join me. I know exactly how to get each of these small bets to $10,000 a month in revenue, for example:

- Five hundred books per month
- Forty hour-long strategy calls
- Two consulting clients
- One course a day

When you start to break down each small bet, you can see a clear path forward to the goal we all want: freedom, independence, and resilience.

The portfolio-of-small-bets approach is one way to achieve that outcome. Every day, more and more people are using the framework to create the life they want for themselves.

CHAPTER 17

How to Budget Your Business Like a Film Producer

Treat your budget as if your customers and clients are depending on you to. Because they are.

One thing I was never taught about business was how to budget. I'd learned how to create a personal budget for myself and then later for my family, and we got it to a point where even though my wife and I are both freelancers with irregular income, we still figured out how to make it work, which included things like buying a house, paying down $20,000 worth of debt in a year, and having some consistency in all the chaos.

What I wish I knew was how to budget my business so that it could survive the ups and downs and ebbs and flows of irregular income, while still paying me a consistent salary every month, remaining profitable, and having enough in the bank to invest and grow.

In this chapter, that's what you'll learn how to do.

How To Budget Like a Film Producer

Feature films are interesting little mini-businesses that start when a chunk of money is given to a production company to make a movie, spent over a matter of months, and then (with hope) turn a profit on the other end. The producer is essentially the CEO of this little (or big) business, and the few movies I've worked on have had budgets that are similar enough to a small or one-person business, like the ones we're trying to build together through this book, to be an appropriate analogy.

Part of my job as a film and TV producer is to create budgets for these films based on how much money is available to spend. If, for example, I am told that we have $750,000 to spend on a movie, it's then my job to give every one of those dollars a "job." This process of allocation is rule number one for budgeting your business.

You, however, might not have film financiers, but you do have clients and customers. My recommendation is to create a budget for the next three months, because who knows how things might change or grow in your business over a longer period of time, like a year. (Two years in a row my business doubled in revenue, which I was not anticipating in my annual budgeting session . . .).

First Determine How Much You Have to Spend

So, take your last three months as a baseline, and assume that you'll make the same amount for the next three months. If you make $7,000 per month, then your total amount to spend is $21,000.

On a film budget, one of the first line items—or jobs for the dollars I have in my budget—is a "contingency" line item. In your budget this would be "profit." Remember, we practice what we preach here, and we take our profit first. So, out of your $21,000, you will take 2, 5, or, 10 percent, whatever amount you've decided on or are working toward. If you've never taken a profit before, set it at 1 or 2 percent.

Now, a quick aside to talk about tools. You don't need expensive software, and there aren't any dedicated business budgeting tools that I've enjoyed using. While I have QuickBooks for my accounting, I am not a fan of the budgeting feature, plus it costs extra. One thing I currently do is I use **YouNeedABudget. com** and tweak it a little for my business so that I can track accounts receivable, but we're getting a bit into the weeds. You can read about how to set it up on their blog, but if you don't want to worry about learning something new, you can use a simple spreadsheet, which is what I'll use for the diagrams and examples in this chapter. Google Sheets even has an Annual Budget Tracker template that you can use that has a bunch of pre-built formulas and some nice design to it as well.

So, you start with what you have to budget, $21,000 in our example, and enter that on the first page of the template.

My Business Budget

Plan and track your monthly spending for the entire year.

How to use this template

1. Get started by entering your starting balance in Row 13 below.

2. Then, fill out the 'Expenses' and 'Income' tabs.

3. Feel free to rename or delete categories in these tabs. Your changes will automatically be reflected on the 'Summary' tab, which shows an overview of your projected/actual spending.

Configure

Starting balance: $21,000

Budget Allocation – Give Every Dollar A Job

Next, you'll want to rename the different budget categories and make the top three profit, taxes, and owner's pay. For this example I'll just use 1 percent for profit.

Expenses		Jan	Feb	Mar
Profit	Monthly totals:	$70	$70	$70
Taxes	Monthly totals:	$1,050	$1,050	$1,050
Owner's Pay	Monthly totals:	$4,000	$4,000	$4,000
		$4,000	$4,000	$4,000

I've got 15 percent of revenue set aside for taxes, and I want to pay myself $4,000 per month in salary. That comes to a total of $15,360, so we have $5,640 left to budget in our Operating Expenses category.

Now it's up to us to decide how to allocate that remaining money. If you've never budgeted before, you can look at your last one to three months of spending and see where your money goes and enter the average amount into that sub-category under operating expenses. Or you can choose how much you want to spend from the different categories you create and then spend accordingly.

The next image shows some typical categories for creative businesses, but you can add or remove to create a budget that makes sense for your business.

Operating Expenses

Monthly totals:
Accounting Services
Advertising & Marketing
Bank Charges & Fees
Coaching
Car & Truck
Contractors
Equipment Purchase
Equipment Rental
Gifts
Insurance
Internet
Job Supplies
Legal & Professional Services
Meals & Entertainment
Location Rentals
Office Supplies
Phone
Professional Development
Shipping
Software & Subscriptions
Travel
Uncategorized OPEX

Now, we can divide the balance of $5,640 by three months to see that we have $1,880 to spend each month in the operating expenses category. You could end up with a budget that looks like this:

Operating Expenses	Monthly totals:	$1,880	$1,880	$1,880
	Accounting Services	$40	$40	$40
	Advertising & Marketing	$100	$100	$100
	Bank Charges & Fees	$25	$25	$25
	Coaching	$250	$250	$250
	Car & Truck	$250	$250	$250
	Contractors	$200	$200	$200
	Equipment Purchase	$100	$100	$100
	Equipment Rental	$50	$50	$50
	Gifts	$25	$25	$25
	Insurance	$40	$40	$40
	Internet	$50	$50	$50
	Job Supplies	$100	$100	$100
	Legal & Professional Services	$25	$25	$25
	Meals & Entertainment	$150	$150	$150
	Location Rentals	$50	$50	$50
	Office Supplies	$50	$50	$50
	Phone	$50	$50	$50
	Professional Development	$100	$100	$100
	Shipping	$25	$25	$25
	Software & Subscriptions	$150	$150	$150
	Travel	$50	$50	$50
	Uncategorized OPEX	$40	$40	$40

It's always good to leave a little buffer in the "uncategorized" subcategory for the inevitable yet unexpected expenses that pop up each month.

Only Spend What You've Allocated

This is the part of budgeting many creatives and solo business owners could improve on, myself included. Here's an example of what we tend to do with our budgets.

An expense comes up, like our hard drive is suddenly full and we have to go get a new one. We check the bank account and see $2,874 in there, which is plenty to go and buy a new hard drive, so we head out to the computer store and get a nice big drive for $400.

Then, a few days later, an invoice for a contractor on our last project is due, for $2,500. But we look at our account and realize there's only $2,474 in there, so we can't pay the invoice on time unless we move some money around. We know that some money is coming in from a client in a few days, so we borrow some money from our personal account, or a credit card, pay the invoice, and are left with no money in our bank account for a few days.

When the client invoice comes in, expenses have been piling up, so we rush to pay off the credit card, replenish our personal account, and then deal with the next bill in the stack. It's all very reactionary, hectic, and stressful.

Now, we need to stop operating this way as quickly as possible. With this new budget in place, we know how much we have to spend on different parts of our business. While we may have $2,874 in our account, we need to look at our budget for the month to see how much money has been spent from the equipment purchases subcategory, and if there's not enough for a $400 hard drive, we don't buy the hard drive.

If that's the case, you can either buy a less expensive drive, wait a month until you've saved enough in that category, or move money from another category to cover the larger expense.

Rather than looking at a single number—the available balance in your bank account—you need to consult your budget, which will give you more context as to how much is available to spend in this specific category right now, how much money is already allocated for other expenses, and how much money is coming in.

Track Your Accounts Receivable

Speaking of money coming in, it's important to stay on top of how much money is coming in over the next few months. This is known as your "accounts receivable," which is the outstanding invoices that have been sent out to clients and customers but haven't yet been paid.

As you're projecting out over the next three months, it's important to know if you're potentially expecting a month where your income is lower than your planned expenses. If that happens, you have two options:

- Cut your expenses for the month
- Make more money

Yes, I know it sounds a little facetious, but I'm being serious. You are the owner of your business, and if you spend more than you make, you're destined for bankruptcy. That's why we want to be profitable from the start, but also profitable for as long as our business exists.

If you set up an accounts receivable tracking system, whether using QuickBooks, YouNeedABudget.com, or your spreadsheet, you'll have months to adapt and take action, rather than reacting to a situation that just happened. If you know you have some big expenses coming up like travel or contractors or purchases, and your income isn't sufficient to cover those increased amounts, then you need to make plans on how you're going to deal with the situation. If you plan to make more money, then come up with a list of ideas on how to get a few more projects, increase sales on the lower-rung projects on your sales ladder, or get paid sooner from a future client. I highly suggest that you avoid things like debt, gap or bridge loans, invoice factoring, or anything else where you're borrowing money to pay for something now, and then having to pay interest later. Think of that debt interest as your profit, and wave goodbye to your profitable business. While 5 to 10 percent interest may seem small, if you're only taking 2 to 5 percent profit in your business, you just spent your profit on paying back that interest. Credit cards are even worse as they can run into the teens and twenties, interest-rate wise, which can dramatically impact the profitability of your business.

On a movie, instead of "categories" I have "departments" — an art department, camera department, production department, and more. (There can be dozens of departments on bigger films). I give each of these departments a budget they have to spend for the movie, and they don't get to go over that budget. If they think they might, it's my job to either prevent that overspending, or move money from other areas of the budget to cover it. On a film, you don't want to have to go back to the financiers and ask for more money. It shows that you didn't budget properly, or anticipate the spend in a timely enough manner. And if you have to go get more money from them, it often comes at a premium— think 15 percent interest or more.

That decision eats into the profitability of the film and makes it harder for the movie to make money through a sale or distribution deal. The same is true for your business. Budgeting is about planning and anticipation. You plan months ahead and allocate money to be spent so that you know you have enough for each category of spending. Then you focus some of your time on a few months ahead and adjust your budget each month, either putting more into profit, cutting expenses, or finding ways to increase your revenue.

I recommend that every quarter you adjust your numbers. See if you can cut your operating expenses a little. Increase how much money you put aside into profit, raising it by 1 percent every quarter until you feel like you have a comfortable amount sitting in that account. Then, you get to do something fun for yourself.

Every quarter, your business is going to pay you a dividend. This is your business giving you a gift for being profitable. Take

50 percent of the amount that you've set aside for profit and pay it to your personal account. This is not income; this is a bonus. You get to spend it on whatever you want—a nice meal with your partner or family, a new watch, a trip, an experience; it's up to you! It's a perk of owning your own business that most creators never afford themselves because they never set aside any profit.

In the first year that I started setting aside money as profit, I bought myself an $80 smart watch, some equipment for a backpacking trip, a new computer screen, and an iPad. Imagine what you would do with a nice $100, $1,000, or even a $10,000 quarterly dividend!

The other nice thing that will happen with you setting aside money for taxes is that you can pay quarterly taxes for both your business and your personal taxes! Your business can take care of you in more ways than one when you budget for it.

Plan out a budget for the next three months. Allocate every dollar by giving it a "job." Track your spending weekly to see how much of each category you've spent, and make sure not to overspend in any category without being able to cover it from another part of your budget. Anticipate one to three months out to see how much you plan to make and how much you plan to spend. Adjust your budget every quarter to set more aside for profit and pay yourself a dividend. Budget your business like a movie, and you'll always have enough to be profitable, and enjoy the benefits of having a business that you're financially managing like a film producer.

PART 4

Marketing and Audience Building Mastery

"People don't buy what you do; they buy why you do it. And what you do simply proves what you believe"
— Simon Sinek, Start with Why: How Great Leaders Inspire Everyone to Take Action

There's a huge difference between the Contractor mindset and the Craftsman mindset when it comes to audience and marketing—one believes that it matters.

During the first decade of my career, my belief was that "if I could just get better at my craft, people will take notice, and I'll get 'picked' to do the jobs I've always wanted to do." The problem with that belief is that it ignores reality. "If you build it, they will come" is a great line for a movie about baseball players coming back from the dead and playing in what was a cornfield, but it doesn't apply to your creative business. More effective would be, "if you build it and then spend just as much energy telling people that you built it and why they should care and how it makes their life better, you might convince a small percentage of them to become customers."

I firmly believe that if I'd had the lessons in this section at the beginning of my career, I could have done in two to three years what took me ten to twelve to accomplish. That's how powerful marketing mastery and the power of an audience is. In the months that I started taking these principles seriously in 2021, I doubled the size of my audience, created a handful of new products specific to their needs, and made more than five figures in revenue, all from assets that didn't exist before I started this process.

In the next twelve months, this new audience will become the basis of my success in Craftsman Creative, and my "portfolio of small bets" will go from five-figure revenues to six-figure revenues, and be positioned to grow to a seven-figure, one-person business in the next two to three years. I've taken what I've learned as well as lessons from those who have been doing marketing and audience building for decades and put it into this section so that you can take the fast track to a sustainable, audience-first creative business that is fulfilling and profitable.

CHAPTER 18

Seven Principles of Marketing for Creators

Shift your mindset around marketing and grow your business like never before

Understanding and applying proven marketing principles and frameworks have changed my business. I know they can change yours, too. Therefore, I expect this section on marketing and audience building might be the most impactful section of the whole book.

In this chapter, I'm going to outline some of the most important principles for you, and in the rest of this section, we'll dive deeper into how to apply those principles in your business to get you the results you want. Specifically: more fans, more followers, more subscribers, and more clients and customers.

Here are my seven most important marketing principles for creators, in no particular order.

1. Marketing Is Required

A business with no marketing is a business without sales.

One of the most important mindset shifts you can make in this area is to take responsibility for the marketing of your business as the business owner. No one else is going to market your business for you—without paying them, at least. If no one knows your business exists, that you made a new piece of art, released a new song, or created a new video, how on earth do you expect anyone to buy it?

Whether it's email marketing, word of mouth, social media, content, or any other type of marketing (we'll get into the different options later in the book), marketing is required for you to go from a five-figure creator to a six-figure business owner.

2. Marketing Isn't Selling

Too many creators shy away from marketing because they don't want to be too "sales-y" with their audience. But, and this is important, marketing is not the same as selling.

The two are completely different parts of your business. While they should work together to create the desired outcome, as any functioning system should, they are not the same.

Marketing is about getting more awareness. It's how people discover that you exist and decide whether they ultimately want to do business with you—or follow you, subscribe to your content, etc. Sales are about conversion. It's how you turn someone who knows about your business into a customer.

Selling is an event. Marketing is a process.

3. Marketing Isn't Advertising

Marketing is how you tell your story to pull the right people into your world and serve them, whether as a subscriber, follower, client, or customer. Advertising is the vehicle used to get your marketing message in front of an audience of people. Again, like sales, marketing and advertising should work hand in hand. We'll talk more about systems later in the book.

But they are not the same. Marketing is the story you want to tell. Advertising is the way to get that story in front of people using paid channels.

For our purposes, we'll refer to advertising as any paid method of getting in front of your audience, using ads or similar channels. Marketing, on the other hand, is free. You can publish content on social media, YouTube, a newsletter, or numerous other places without spending any money at all.

Tesla, notoriously, **doesn't spend money on ads**, and yet they have grown to become the world's most valuable carmaker.

If they can grow to nearly a **trillion-dollar market cap** and billions a year in sales with no advertising, you can certainly reach six figures in your business.

4. To Do Marketing Well, You Need to Understand Your Audience

Effective marketing is not a "spray and pray" process. Instead, effective marketing means targeting a specific audience and delivering value that helps them in some way.

When you market a video production company to an audience of product makers who need videos for their business, you are providing value. You're making it easier for them to promote their products using your services.

When you share your music online and tell people about the song, how it will make them feel, how they may connect with the lyrics, you're helping people have an experience that they wouldn't have otherwise.

All this leads to this principle:

It's much easier to market to someone who is already looking for what you have than to try and convince someone that they need what you make.

We'll use this principle throughout this section as a foundation to build on. Spending time trying to convince people is expensive and time-consuming, and rarely leads to the desired outcome of a new client or customer.

In 2015 and 2016 I spent months, easily over one hundred hours of my time, trying to raise money for a feature film. The approach I took was to connect with, or "market to," venture capital firms here in Utah.

It was easy enough to find a directory of dozens of firms with lots of money, so I went through and found the emails of people who worked at the different firms and sent cold emails—a form of outbound marketing. Hundreds of emails led to dozens of responses and a handful of in-person meetings where I could share the "marketing message" of the investment opportunity.

Yet, meeting after meeting ended with the same response: "This sounds amazing, and you pitched the project well, but we simply can't invest."

Wait, what? Why not?

Turns out that venture capital firms have a very strict box that contains the types of things they can invest in. And none of the boxes at any of these firms contained "feature films." As good as the investment was, and no matter how well I pitched it, there was simply no convincing these firms to invest because they were bound through their agreements to only invest in specific industries. All that wasted time could have been avoided if I knew this one thing going in.

It's easier to market to people who are already looking for what you have than to try and convince someone to work with you. Funnily enough, the money we did end up raising came from someone who emailed us about the project because they had heard about our project and wanted to learn more.

We'll go into much more detail about the importance and process of understanding your audience later in this section.

5. Marketing Is Easy When It Is Connected to Your Purpose

Early in 2021, I kept seeing everyone on Twitter join in this thirty-day challenge to write every day for thirty days. The #Ship-30for30 hashtag was all over my feed.

I looked at the program and decided I didn't need to spend $400 or whatever the price was to write every day for thirty days and publish it as a screenshot. So I decided to just do it myself! I started writing every day about finance and even had some good results from it. Yet, after 11 days I stopped writing.

The reason is that I hadn't connected this content marketing effort to my bigger purpose with Craftsman Creative. Compare that to this book, which you're now reading but was largely written in public, which the first drafts shared and serialized multiple times a week.

I've consistently shown up, day after day, working on the book and publishing new chapters. The reason it worked this time around? Because it's a book that connects so easily and clearly to the greater purpose and vision I have for my business.

The book helps me reach new people, welcomes more people into the world of Craftsman Creative, and creates the platform—the "minimum viable audience"—for future success. When everything is in alignment with a bigger purpose and vision, things not only become easier to do, but how it all fits together becomes clearer. It feels more like a complete thought than a random set of marketing messages every day. And that's what good writing is: clear and focused thinking about something that matters to you.

6. Marketing Is Service. It's Contribution.

When you shift your thinking from marketing being "salesy" and gross to it being a service to the people you hope to one day have as clients, everything changes. The words you use. The stories you tell. The frequency and timing and the way that you put those messages in front of people. It all shifts. People don't get turned off. They get pulled in.

A short example from my early attempts at marketing Craftsman Creative on Twitter. I saw a tweet from someone I'd never met or interacted with before about feeling nervous as she was going into a negotiation with a brand who wanted to bring her on as a marketing manager. I gave a few responses in the tweets, and then let her know I was happy to answer more questions if she wanted to message me directly.

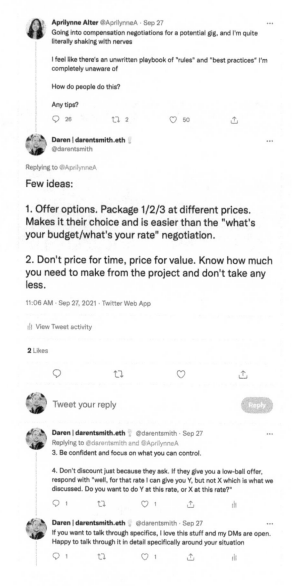

That conversation continued, I even recorded a short Loom video to go over the philosophy around negotiations and pricing. She then started asking about my work, and the book that I was writing—the very book you're reading now—and offered to help promote it.

Nearly three months later and she was one of the first three people to sign up for early access to the book and the community, I've purchased a Twitter header NFT from her that is now the image at the top of my weekly newsletter, and we interact often on Twitter, supporting each other's work.

When you serve people and show up as yourself online, people get pulled in.

That being said, marketing is just as much about pulling the right people in as it is about clearly keeping the "wrong" people out. I knew I had succeeded at this with the subtitle for this book, which is a type of marketing message: "Helping five-figure creators build six-figure businesses"

This book isn't to help people who are making a million a year grow their business to $10 million a year. It's not for startups that are trying to scale and grow to an exit. It's not for investors who want to better understand the creator economy.

Could those people benefit from the principles in this book? Probably. But if they were to purchase the book in hopes of getting their needs met, they would likely be disappointed and leave a one-star review.

Your marketing is a promise that says that those who engage with this thing you made will get something valuable. In this case, the five-figure (and even one-, two-, three-, and four-figure) creators who read this book will learn how to create six-figure businesses. That's the promise that I'm delivering. And that's the expectation that my readers are bringing to their experience with the book.

Clarity helps your audience, those who aren't your audience, and you as the marketer.

7. There Isn't One Right Way to Market to Your Audience

Always remember that the goal with marketing isn't to discover the one objectively correct way to market to your audience. Perfect doesn't exist.

Marketing is a process, one that evolves over time the more you analyze and improve it. You'll experiment with different things. Some will work. Some won't. Do more of what works and less of what doesn't, and you can't help but get better at marketing.

If you see it as a series of experiments, rather than a search for the holy grail, you'll make the process much easier on yourself. There is, however, one principle that will help you discover the things that work much faster.

Get permission first.

Seth Godin's book Permission Marketing was a game-changer when it was first published. It was during the time when marketers were ruining the internet with all sorts of cheap and interrupting messages because clicks were cheap and the internet was the wild, wild west. Anything went, so to speak.

But Seth's "permission marketing" framework has stood the test of time. Getting permission from people before you begin marketing to them ensures that only the people who want to be marketed to receive those messages. Everyone else can keep getting value from you without ever feeling marketed to. It's a beautiful approach that carries the utmost respect for your audience.

More on permission marketing later, but important for now to consider what this principle would look like for your marketing and the way you treat your audience.

In the rest of this section, we'll cover many other principles that will, with hope, shift your mindset and help you succeed at marketing. Principles that treat your audience with respect, give them incredible amounts of value and help you grow your audience in ways that you haven't been able to before, providing you with an incredible platform for future success.

CHAPTER 19

Grow Awareness and Trust Through Your Marketing

*The product first versus audience first
argument is a false choice*

Which comes first? The audience? Awareness? The product?

Where do you start when you're thinking about marketing? Many people will say that "the product should market itself," but how exactly do you do that? Is there a proven method to it all?

Well, not that I've found.

In this chapter, however, I'll cover what I've learned from fifteen years of having to wear the "marketing hat" in my businesses, and what's worked for myself and others in creative industries.

The Chicken and the Egg of Marketing

Audience first or product first, that seems to be the question.

Do you set out to record an album then hope to find the audience for it? Or spend years and years writing and performing songs to see what resonates and what audience forms around your music?

My belief is that it's a false dichotomy. There aren't only two options. As stated in the chapter on Vision, the very first thing to determine is your vision, because your vision informs everything else. It will help you understand the makeup of the audience you seek to serve. It will help inform the products or creative works that will best serve and change that audience in a way that fulfills you.

The alternative is to be calculating and opportunistic, jumping on every trend, changing and morphing yourself to whatever you think people will like, and never being fulfilled because you're not being who you are.

Before you start writing songs, or taking photos, or sharing your work with a potential audience, you need to understand who you are and what you're trying to do through your work. It may feel like a tall order, but don't stress. There's no right answer, and you're not going to be judged or graded by people. The only metric to measure is how aligned your work feels with your greater vision and purpose.

There's No Right Answer

Let's deconstruct this dichotomy.

I've seen plenty of people record an album or do a **photography project** before thinking about the intended audience to great success. Does that mean you should create the product first? The startup world will tell you, "No! You have to build an audience first!" So then people set out to build an audience first and have massive success as well. But people seeing that success try to duplicate it and chase after the audience first without any connection to their vision, and they end up with an audience of fans but not customers.

Then what's the answer? Tell me! I can't. There is no one right answer.

I've written online for more than a decade. I've started businesses and blogs and self-published books, but never to any amount of success. Yet my own experience has taught me that pursuing what fulfilled me, something that aligned with my greater vision for my life and my businesses, and putting it out there consistently is what ultimately worked.

While my audience is still small in comparison to some, the signals are there that are showing me what is and isn't working, and that process provides a compass of where I'm headed and what to do next.

The Importance of Awareness

Now that I've been sufficiently vague about answering the product/audience first conundrum, let's focus on what matters.

Awareness.

I've heard Seth Godin say this no less than a dozen times:

You don't have a product problem. You have an awareness problem.

Whether you focus on audience or product first, in order to succeed you need to have some level of awareness. Meaning— people know your work exists. Audience size is fairly irrelevant, because depending on the product you could sell **just one thing** and be set for life. If you happened to find that one customer in an audience of ten or one hundred, all the better, because you didn't have to spend as much time growing a huge audience.

Is the artist with an audience of one hundred people but annual revenues of $10 million a success or a failure? It depends on how you measure it.

But there are plenty of examples of influencers over the years who have built large audiences and yet struggle to have a profitable business. Are they successful because of the audience size despite not having a resilient business model? Again, it depends on how you measure it.

Determine the Size of Your Minimum Viable Audience

What we want to get to in our businesses is a place where we have that "minimum viable audience," the smallest number of people that can support our work and allow us the freedom to do our creative work full time. Generally speaking, a business that can pay us $100,000 a year in salary.

The size of your minimum viable audience will be determined by the products or services you sell, and how much you sell them for. You may only need one client at $10,000 per month. Or you may need one thousand people to pay you $120 a year. Or ten thousand people who will buy your $12 album every year.

If you're an author selling books and you make $5 per sale, to make $10,000 a month for your business you need to sell 2,000 books a month.

Pretty straightforward. But here's where a lot of creators get stuck:

If 20 percent of your audience will buy your book,
then you need 10,000 people for your first month,
and you'll need to add 10,000 more people per month
to continue selling 2,000 books per month.

(And we wonder why writers struggle to make enough money. They never take the time to learn and accept these realities, nor do they charge enough for their books.)

If you're a graphic designer who charges $2,500 per project, you need four projects a month.

Maybe 2 percent of your audience will buy.

4 projects ÷ 2 percent = 200 people per month.

That can be traffic to your website, new followers on social media, or new subscribers to your newsletter, but the metrics are the reality that will determine your minimum viable audience. Not just your current audience, but the size of the audience you need to attract each and every month.

You may be able to start with 200 people, but if you're not adding 200 more people per month, you won't get 4 projects or $10,000 until you either grow your audience or get better at selling a larger percentage of people, which we'll discuss in the section on selling.

This is why marketing is so important. For you to succeed, you need to either have a way for the same customers to purchase from you more often (annually, monthly, bi-annually, etc.), and/or find new people every month to purchase from you.

This is why SaaS—or Software As A Service—businesses like Netflix are so successful. You pay a monthly amount to keep your subscription and access active.

Every month, Netflix knows that 100M or so people are going to pay them on average $12. That's $1.2 billion dollars every month that they can more or less count on.

At that point, they have two goals—keep current subscribers happy so they don't cancel their subscription and add new customers to grow their business.

You can do the same on a smaller scale.

What are jobs to be done that you can do for $5-$100 per month? Can you start a paid newsletter, a paid community, a monthly zoom call where you teach your craft, release an exclusive-to-subscribers product?

Patreon capitalized on this success and created a platform to help artists and creators build this model into their business. You can create tiers for different levels of access or content that automatically charges your audience every month.

Plenty of creators have built audiences of thousands of patrons who want that very specific job to be done every month, and now make tens or even hundreds of thousands of dollars per month through that platform.

Even platforms like YouTube use this similar model. You grow an audience of subscribers and then monetize your videos, and you know that some percentage of your audience is going to watch your video every week within the first few days it's released. Anything beyond that from people sharing it or the algorithm putting it in front of new audiences is a bonus.

If you know you're going to get 100,000 views every week from your audience, and that represents $1,000 of ad revenue, then you know that growing your audience to where 250,000 people view your video every week means you're making $10,000 per month from weekly videos. ($2,500 per week x four weeks).

Delivering on a Promise

Your marketing efforts are a promise that you're making to your current and potential audience.

"If you listen to this music, you will feel better"

"These photographs will look great in your home or office"

"My design work will elevate your brand"

"My coaching will help improve your life"

These messages are implicit rather than explicit, though I guess you could just outright say what you are trying to say. "Watermelons for sale" is a perfect message for someone who wants to buy watermelons. But "My new album is out today" probably doesn't have the same effect on an audience who doesn't yet know you or trust in your music's ability to help them feel the way they want to feel.

That marketing message might work on your existing audience, but in order to grow your audience, you need to get the awareness of people who don't yet know you exist. The messages to that group of people need to include more context and help them understand how your work will change them. You're not a commodity like a watermelon. You're a creator. An artist. A maker. A builder. The way you gain awareness for your work should help people understand what will change if they engage with it.

It wasn't until I landed on the marketing message that's the subtitle of this book that things started to click and work for me, and my audience started to grow.

"How five-figure creators can build six-figure businesses."

There is clarity on who it's for and what it does. Simple and straightforward.

You Audience Becomes Your Compass

Once you've connected an audience and a vision and start creating for them (in whatever order you see fit), what's amazing is that the audience becomes a compass you can use to guide your way.

Justin Welsh is someone I've met through Twitter who has grown a massive audience on both LinkedIn and Twitter. He recently **shared this thread** about building and monetizing an audience by solving the problems the audience had:

Justin Welsh
@JustinSaaS

Last week my little one-person business crossed $1.3M in revenue.

It took 810 days, I ran zero paid ads and operate at a ~98% margin.

Here are the 14 steps of my strange journey:

Hope it's helpful to someone.

[thread]

10:04 AM · Oct 26, 2021 · Hypefury

718 Retweets   **83** Quote Tweets   **5,860** Likes

Part of the steps that Justin outlines in that thread is that the audience told him what they wanted from him, and he made it.

Now, if you're an artist or a musician this approach may be too calculated. You don't always want your audience to tell you what music to write. But you will start to see what music resonates with them the most. What songs are people singing along to at your shows? Which ones get the most streams on Spotify? That could help you decide on what tone to use in the next album, or what topics work best.

My friend Faith Marie realized early on that the more she wrote about her anxiety or depression or struggles with mental health, the more she connected with her audience that finally felt like an artist understood what they were going through. Faith had started singing songs at a local venue when she was in her early teens, and by the time she was fifteen or sixteen she was writing incredible songs with deep, moving lyrics. I was hired to film a music video for her song "Antidote," and listened to the song a few times and then again as I was driving up to the location.

As I listened to the song on the way up, I nearly cried because I couldn't believe a girl so young could have such incredible emotion and connection through her music. We made **this music video**, and it's now been viewed more than five million times, because she connected with an audience who then shared her music and helped her gain more awareness.

My friends Alan and Jono started a YouTube channel that blew up in 2020 because people needed help with the emotional struggle of being quarantined and losing jobs and everything else. Their channel, **Cinema Therapy**, has grown to nearly one million subscribers in just under eighteen months.

Both of these are examples of creators making something that they were passionate about and then getting it in front of the right audience through their marketing.

Their work delivers on the promise. Faith's song helps you feel better. Alan & Jono's channel helps bring clarity to your life and helps you feel better. They both cause a change in their audience.

The more they create, the more their audience grows, and the more feedback they get on what's working and what isn't. They can then choose to do more of the same or expand out from there depending on what their audience compass is showing them.

How To Start Marketing to Your Audience Like A Craftsman

The important thing at this moment is to start. Wherever you are, however large or small your following, you can take steps to improve your marketing and gain more awareness for the work you're doing. Here is a non-exhaustive list of things you could do right now:

- Connect your work to your vision and purpose
- Take time to understand the change you hope to affect in people
- Share what you're making with the people you hope to change
- See if it works
- If yes, do more of the same
- If no, either keep going and try a different angle, or experiment with new ideas or new ways to get awareness.

One thing I can tell you is that you'll never gain a minimum viable audience if you never share your work. The audience has to have something to become aware of, which means you need to be creating often and sharing often. There's no such thing as perfect marketing. As Sahil Lavingia says in his book The Minimalist Entrepreneur: How Great Founders Do More with Less, "you don't learn, then start. You start, then learn."

The more consistently you show up and take action, the more people will become aware of your work and join you on the creative journey. Without sharing, you never give people an opportunity to benefit from your products and services. Once you do, the people who see the value will come, and they'll tell others if your work is worthy of recommendation. It all compounds once you find a marketing approach that works. Sometimes that experimentation can take a few months; other times it may take years. But if you have connected your work to a greater purpose, you'll have the resilience and grit to keep going and not give up too early.

Patience is an important quality to cultivate. Many creators, myself included, struggle with going directly from desired result to action, skipping over the purpose. But your actions, if you want to sustain them through the ups and downs of being a creative, need to be connected to your purpose and your vision. Too many people give up too early, and much of the success you'll realize in your career and in your business will come because you kept going far after the initial feeling of "this is pointless."

Even Albert Einstein once credited much of his success to his ability to stick with a problem more so than his intelligence. "It's not that I'm so smart," the physicist said, "it's just that I stay with problems longer."

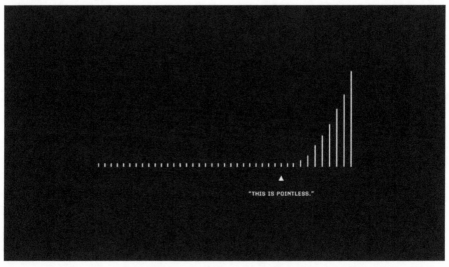

Image by Jack Butcher, Visualize Value

CHAPTER 20

Identify Jobs to Be Done

*Understand what your audience wants—and
why they want it—better than they do.*

Often, we approach creating something by starting with the question, "what do I want to create?" While that works great for artists, the downside is that it can take longer to resonate with an audience of people.

If our goal is to create for an audience of people who want what we're selling, that's less a process of creation and more of a process of discovery.

Plenty of people have talked about **Clayton Christensen's "Jobs To Be Done"** theory, including myself. Here's a quick breakdown of the "Jobs To Be Done" theory:

People don't simply buy products or services, they "hire" them to make progress in specific circumstances.

Said differently, when you understand the reason that a client or customer is hiring you for—the "job to be done"—you can serve them better. When we take what we've learned in earlier chapters, we can use this theory to form a different perspective around audience building. We can reverse engineer an audience using this principle to get to a minimum viable audience as quickly as possible. Once we know what jobs they want to hire us for, we can eliminate all of the other guessing and building products and features they don't care about, and focus directly on the most impactful work. This, in turn, serves them better and they gain an affinity for you as someone they can trust to do that job again

The Goal of Audience Building

The point of building an audience isn't just to inflate some vanity metric like subscribers, followers, views, or likes, even though that's what you see most people pursue.

> **"I'm only 45 followers away from 10k! Who's gonna help me hit this huge milestone?!"**

The point is to discover what jobs the audience needs done and align that with the creative work you seek to do.

Take our example musician again. They, like any other artist, create a different album every two years.

In one scenario, they create whatever music speaks to them in the moment. It's about them, what they're going through, a reflection on their current life experiences. With this approach, every album is a different genre—a departure for the audience that has discovered them so far and has enjoyed their music in the past.

The other option is to evolve, not depart. In this scenario, the artist realizes the genre buckets that people put her in, but more importantly, the jobs to be done that her audience has. She asks, "Do they connect with my lyrics? My tone? My voice? The genre?" What do they get when they listen to my music? Are they uplifted? Contemplative? Blown away? Energized? Connected?

If she grew her audience by writing contemplative, lyrical, melodic acoustic music over three albums, and then came out with an experimental math rock album with no lyrics at all, how many fans would follow her to this new place and purchase the new album?

Instead, she decides to take what she knows about her audience and the "job they are hiring her for" to slowly evolve her music to that place, rather than departing in one fell swoop.

In this way, she continues to serve the audience that she has as well as expand her audience by branching out slowly to new genre places in her music.

Your goal in growing an audience is to discover the jobs to be done and then become the first person that comes to mind when that audience needs that job done.

Over fifteen years in the film industry in Utah, I went from being a post-production sound guy to a writer to a producer. It wasn't until after eight years as a producer that people started hiring me without me knowing who they were. It was the first signal of becoming "the guy" who can get the job of "producing" done for that audience of people. Eleven years in I was asked, seemingly out of the blue, to produce a feature film directed by Amy Redford.

But it wasn't out of the blue.

To that small audience of Amy and her business partner, I had worked with them for over two years to become the first "guy" they thought of to produce their movie. They needed someone to handle the budget, the logistics, hiring and taking care of the crew, and getting this movie made. I was the only one they asked because I was "the guy." All I needed at that moment was an audience size of two.

The experience of producing the movie expanded my audience. I worked with people on the movie who then recommended me to others and became better friends with the people working at the Utah Film Commission and the Utah Film Studios, who began to see me as "the guy" as well.

The more my audience grew—from one to two, to five, to ten, to fifty—the easier it became to have work come to me rather than having to go out and convince people to hire me. I built the audience, and the audience hired me for the job. Perfect alignment from the start because I added people to my audience that I knew I wanted to serve and could deliver on the job. I no longer had to search for jobs every time I needed money because enough demand was coming directly from the audience I'd built.

This is the dream scenario we all wish for.

As I write this, it's November 1, 2021. As of last week, I'd already lined up three feature films to produce next year, all from my audience. If the average fee is $30,000, then my whole year is basically covered, with two months left before 2022 even starts.

Think about how much financial stress that removes knowing that I'm not going to have to chase work next year! Anything else that comes into my world beyond that is a bonus, and I'll have the freedom to say yes or no to each project.

I've found a "minimum viable audience" for my producing work. I can only do two to three movies a year because each takes around four months to produce, so from here I'll start increasing my fees to $40K, $50K, $75K and beyond per film by saying no to the smaller budget movies and moving into $2 to 5M features and then $5 to $10M features. Same amount of work, more income.

All I need to do from here is expand that minimum viable audience to include other filmmakers who are making bigger-budget movies. I'm just expanding the audience to include more of the same people, just at a different scale, but they all share one thing—the same "job to be done."

One other example, for good measure, because it shows that you can use jobs to be done theoretically to serve two or even more audiences with a single product or service.

Reverse Engineer the Audience You Want to Have

Jeremy Chou is a wedding photographer who has been featured in wedding publications worldwide. The reason he's been so successful is that he understood the job to be done for these publications.

They needed pretty people in expensive, exclusive locations to grace the pages of their magazines—that's the "job to be done."

Pretty people getting married in expensive, exclusive locations needed an experienced photographer to capture their wedding day through photos—that's their "job to be done."

Jeremy understood the jobs to be done of two different audiences—wedding clients and wedding publications—but built his business to accommodate both with his work.

What's more, Jeremy set out to be a photographer but combined his experience as an architect to deliver a unique, one-of-a-kind style of photography.

Over the first years of his business, he methodically grew his audience to include these publications and clients that would allow him to deliver this very specific job to be done at a high level to satisfy both groups.

Now he raises his rates every year and travels the world doing luxury wedding photography and continues to get free awareness for his brand by getting published regularly.

You can't have a business without an audience of people who have a job to be done, a "minimum viable audience."

The great thing about this is it changes the audience definition from one of demographics—"women ages 35-49," "men with $250k+ in annual income living in San Francisco, Los Angeles, or New York," etc.—to one of psychographics.

Psychographics are easier to find online because people post and search for their jobs to be done every day.

Head over to Quora or Twitter or Reddit or look at Google Search results. People even tell you the exact language they use to find someone to do this job that they need to be done.

Once you identify your job to be done, you then can find your minimum viable audience.

If you want to sell low-budget horror screenplays to producers, you need to find the fifty to one hundred producers who are hiring screenwriters for that job and become the first person they think of when they need to hire someone.

If you want to hand-letter signage for local businesses, you need to build an audience of local business owners who love your work and need that job to be done.

Here's the framework, broken down step-by-step:

- What is the job to be done that you want to be known for?

- Who are the people that are going to hire you for that job?

- How many times a year do you need to do that job to have a six-figure business?

- What percentage of your audience will hire you for that job?

- How large does your audience have to be to have a minimum viable audience?

In the next chapter, we'll look at how to determine the size of your minimum viable audience.

CHAPTER 21

Marketing for Creatives: Pull, Not Push

The goal of your marketing is not to push people to a sale as quickly as possible

This is one of those ideas that I wish I'd learned early on in my creative career. It would have saved me more than a decade of grief trying to figure out "how to do marketing," and I can't even begin to imagine where I'd be now. But, as with every principle that you learn, rather than be frustrated that you didn't learn it sooner, it's better to be grateful that you're learning it now.

Here's the big idea:

The goal of your marketing is not to push people to a sale as quickly as possible. It's to create tension that pulls people in who want to be pulled in.

There was a time a few years ago that I was so frustrated that I hadn't yet "figured things out." I felt like I was doing everything right but still not getting the results I wanted in my business and my life.

So, I went searching for an answer, a solution. My "current reality" at the time was frustration, despair, and desperation. I desperately needed to change that reality. I had done enough research and analysis of my problem to know that I wanted to hire a business coach who could help me with both my personal life and the growth of my business. I called a few different coaching programs—E-Myth, Strategic Coach, and Tony Robbins—to shop around and see which would be the best fit.

I knew I had found the solution when the person I was talking to at Tony Robbins Business Results Coaching started describing my current reality even better than I could, and then uncovered a world on the other side that I had only hoped existed. I remember pouring out my frustrations: that I felt like I should have figured all of this out by now, that I wanted to control the future of my business, and that I wanted to get the clarity of how to do that. That's when she explained how coaching could get me the kind of life I wanted. One where I had all of the control and freedom and independence I'd described. It quickly became clear that I had found what I was looking for: someone to fill the job I needed to get done. It was crazy to see that all this time this option existed; I just didn't know how or where to look for it.

It was a massive perspective shift. I went from believing the world was one way to realizing that I only saw a small part of what was possible.

Now, given that situation, how easy was it for me to purchase coaching? I didn't hesitate at all, because it was exactly what I was looking for. To date, it's the largest investment I've made in myself and my business, but it continuously pays back multiple times more value than the dollars I've paid for it.

That's what you want to do with your marketing.

When people discover you, you want them to have the feeling, "where has this been all my life?!"

At that moment, you've created tension. There is now a gap between where they are and where they want to be, and that tension needs to be released. That tension pulls people into your world, rather than the alternative of pushing people to a sales conversation as quickly as possible.

Pull, not push.

Have you ever had a similar experience? Think about the moments in your life when a product, service, or idea has found you at the seemingly perfect time. I'm guessing you didn't feel steered into those situations, but pulled into something that made too much sense to ignore.

On my desk, I keep a spring from a trampoline we had in our backyard that wore out. (We do have three boys, and they're out there nearly every day).

(Please ignore the dirty keyboard…)

I wanted some daily reminder of the importance of creating tension in everything that I write and all of the content that I put out into the world.

Through your marketing, the best way that I've found to bring people into your world is to create tension. It's not about having a "hooky" headline, or great copy on a landing page, or a perfectly optimized funnel.

At this stage, you don't want to think of funnels. You want to think of tension. Creating tension can be as simple as sharing results that you've helped your customers and clients receive. Testimonials, results, outcomes—these are all easy to share with the world in a way that creates the tension of I want those results too! for the right people.

Teasers are another form of tension. Sharing a snippet of a song, a work in progress of a project, or a chapter from an upcoming book will create the tension of I want more of this! in your audience.

There's a reason why every movie on the planet creates teasers and trailers. The whole intent is to create tension. Before seeing the trailer, you didn't know the movie existed, or what it was about, or who was in it. But once you watch the trailer—if they did a proper job—you now have to resolve that tension by seeing the movie.

Being active on social media isn't marketing. Marketing is the process of pulling people into your world by helping them relieve the tension that you've created.

Build in Public to Create Tension

Once you know the jobs to be done that you want to do, then you need to find the audience that is paying for that job to be done.

One of the best things you can do as a creator is to "build in public," which can be described simply:

Show people that you currently do this job successfully for others.

This means sharing the process of doing and creating your work with an audience of interested people, many of whom might become clients if you create tension.

This book started out as a form of building in public, as its first iteration was written publicly. I shared the chapters as I wrote them, and it created tension in the readers to want to read the next chapter.

Photographers can share sneak to Instagram previews from their phone of a shoot that they did that they'll publish on their blog. Those interested in seeing more—resolving the tension of the teaser—will go visit the blog and subscribe.

Musicians can share music videos on YouTube that tease a new album, or even do a live stream of a work in progress, and direct people to follow them if they want to hear the full song when it's recorded.

There are platforms for every type of creator—Medium or blogs for writers, Instagram for artists and photographers, Behance for designers and creators, IndieHackers for makers and developers, and the list goes on. Sharing your process with a community of people helps you grow your audience by creating tension.

The thing to remember is that it's not just about posting randomly. It's about consciously creating tension by creating a gap between people's current reality and their desired reality, where they have the thing that you make or have the outcome that you promise through your services.

Tyler Rye is a photographer who does adventure elopement photography.

The way he managed to do this exclusively was to go from a "I'll take any photo any time" photographer to a photographer that only does adventure elopements.

If you look at his social feed and his website, all you see is proof that he is able to deliver on that very specific job to be done.

Every time he does his work, he posts about it, sharing the results he got for someone else.

Naturally, if you want photos of you and your spouse on the edge of a cliff, Tyler is the guy that you call. You may not even know that you want photos of you and your spouse on the edge of a cliff, but you may suddenly find that desire when you come upon one of his images.

Tyler Rye on Instagram

He's amassed a massive following of 55k+ people, and has a thriving business that has expanded from photography to workshops, **online courses**, and expeditions.

Building his audience by showing his work allowed him to discover new jobs to be done that he could either accept or reject depending on the goals he has for his life and his business.

Share What You Learn Along the Way

Building in public often includes sharing your struggles, the lessons learned, the opportunities you discovered from doing the work.

But the most important aspect is to show the results.

Andrew Gazdeki created the website **MicroAcquire** to help creators sell their businesses with as little friction as possible. Multiple times a week he shares another successful acquisition that came through his platform, reinforcing that his company is the best company for the job to be done of selling your company / acquiring a business.

Hayley Barry is my favorite example of building in public. While still in school at Utah Valley University she started sharing her hand-lettering work online.

She'd design a birthday card, an invitation, a poster. She would take a phrase and design it in her own style of hand lettering.

Soon she created an audience that loved her work. She expanded it by getting more involved in our small city of Provo, Utah. She partnered with local events to design posters.

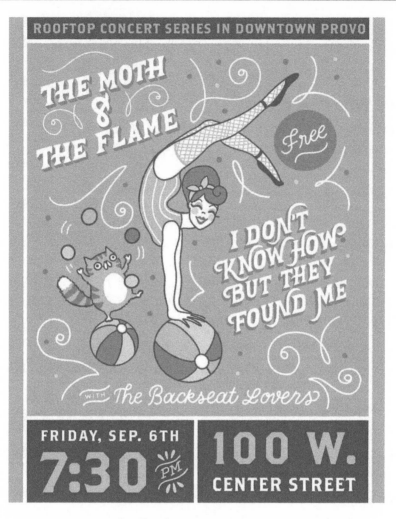

Rooftop Concerts on Instagram

She did a project with a well-known local photographer, Justin Hackworth, to highlight Provo-natives doing awesome things.

People of Provo on Instagram

All of this expanded her audience to the point where she started getting hired for the job she was already doing—hand lettering. People would hire her to create or hand-letter logos in their shops, on walls, and on murals.

The school she was attending put out a request for quotes for a big marketing campaign, and Hayley won the bid. They didn't even know she was still a student at the school, because her work was so good and she had become THE hand-lettering artist in Utah to hire for those jobs.

She then expanded her audience more and started getting hired by national brands and businesses in other parts of the country.

Her audience started asking her to teach them how to do hand-lettering as well, so she created workshops and then an **online course**. In the first weeks of her course launch, she enrolled students from all over the world in over two-dozen countries.

That's the process. Decide the job you want to be known for. Find and connect with an audience who wants to hire you for that job by building in public. Become the person people want to hire for that job. Rinse and repeat.

Building in public can be nerve-wracking for some, but that anxiousness can be alleviated when it's put into the proper perspective.

The best part about building in public is that it's a simple way for you to put out into the world what you're doing and what you're learning, your thoughts and feelings on your work and your industry, and let the people who resonate with that join you in the journey.

Showing a side of yourself that is less polished and less calculated makes it easier for people to feel that affinity toward you, which is what will pull them into your world and get them excited to be a part of it.

CHAPTER 22

Create Products Based on Your Audience's Needs

*Let your audience show you the jobs
that they want to hire you for*

You've identified the "jobs to be done" for an audience you seek to serve, and you've started building in public to show that you're capable of doing those jobs.

Now what?

To start or grow a business from here is a process of listening and observation and analysis, and in this chapter, I'll show you the signals to look for that reveal the products you can create to best serve your audience's needs.

The Signals to Listen For

It wasn't until I started taking this all seriously that I started to see these signals, but when they started to show up it was clear that I was on to something.

Whether you write a newsletter, post on social media, or are simply building in public and sharing your work, you'll start to see signals that show you that you're doing things right.

For years I struggled to grow an audience and write consistently. It wasn't until 2021 that I decided to grow both my email list through my newsletter and **free content** and my **Twitter following** to get more awareness.

The reason I chose those two channels is that it's become clear in the last year how much easier it is to have a successful career as a creator if you have a minimum viable audience.

When I realized this, I did not have a minimum viable audience. I had nearly 1,000 followers on Twitter, but those had accumulated over the 12 years that I'd been on the platform, and my guess is that most of those followers were either bots or inactive or both.

My email list was in a similar state. I had grown it to about 1,000 subscribers, but that was a combination of people that came to events, people who signed up for email series in the past, and those that were interested in what I was writing now.

I had maybe 400-500 people that were actively reading.

Here's how I knew I did not have a minimum viable audience:

In 2020 I started craftsmancreative.co, an online course platform for creators. I began with two of my own courses, and proceeded to tell my audience, "hey! I made this thing for you that I know is valuable and I know you'll like!"

Except, they didn't find it valuable, nor did they like it.

I managed to sell less than 10 people on those courses during the launch. Half of those were "pay what you want" pricing at 50-80% off.

The audience was too minimal to be viable.

So, what are the signals that you're looking for? Let's look at a few:

People Who Are Subscribed Engage with Your Content

You can measure this as a ratio or a percentage, but ideally, you want to be at 50% or more.

Meaning, if you have 100,000 YouTube subscribers, you can count on 50,000 or more of them viewing your videos every week.

If you have a 1,000 person email list, you have a 50% open rate (which is changing because of how Apple is allowing emailing tracking on their phones and computers, but you get the idea).

If you have 5,000 followers on social media, you want to see 2,500+ impressions every time you post new content.

Your Audience Is Reaching Out to You Directly with Questions

This just started happening to me this year when I took my newsletter and Twitter more seriously. I made it easy for people to reply to the emails and left my DMs (direct messages) open on Twitter so that anyone could message me, not just the people I follow.

> If you have "brutal honest" truth to share...let me have it.
>
> I'd love feedback from you on:
>
> What do you think I need to learn?
>
> What is the best way you think I might learn that?
>
> What would be the aprox cost value for that learning?
>
> Thanks,
> Stacey
>
> Oct 20, 2021, 11:32 AM

Every day I get new people messaging me that I've never met or interacted with before. Some have been following me for a day or a week, some for years.

These inquiries then turn into conversations where I'm able to ask questions, learn more about them and what they're doing, and most importantly what they're struggling with.

Margaret Ryland
@MargaretRyland

 Awesome thanks Daren!

Yesterday, 9:57 AM

> Thank you! Means a lot that you'd sign up :)
>
> Yesterday, 11:53 AM ✓

My pleasure. I'm eagerly wanting to learn about web3 and am already an avid reader of your book/blog so was excited to see your announcement!

 Thank YOU for writing about it! 😊

Yesterday, 12:57 PM

> What's your biggest question right now?
>
> Yesterday, 12:58 PM ✓

Not so much a question but my biggest challenge is getting past a massive mental block/fear of creating. Because I know the area I'm moving into is new territory so my first efforts won't be perfect. Which hurts my perfectionist soul 😂

 I'm working through The Artist's Way and the morning pages have been revolutionary. (I think you also do them right?)

Yesterday, 12:59 PM

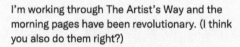
> Yes I do! Have for years. Well good, this content is aimed to help creators, but it's helpful to know that I should address the fear of starting something new. Thanks so much for that insight!

Yesterday, 1:42 PM ✓

This week alone I've been able to have amazing conversations with two people who I connected with months ago, who are so great at replying to the content I put out there.

In these messages are clues or signals as to what I could create in the future to best serve their needs.

From long conversations with these two wonderful ladies over the last few months, I have two "super fans" who are reading everything I write, as well as asking about working with me directly.

They shared their struggles, what they were actively looking for—their "jobs to be done"—and that can inform what I do in the future, from the content I write to the courses I produce, and the community and coaching products that I'm planning on building in 2022.

When you start getting regular replies to your newsletters and direct messages on social media, that's a sign that people are starting to look to you as someone who can help with their "jobs to be done."

People Share Your Work with Their Audiences

This is one of the strongest signals to look for when you're trying to grow your audience, not just serve the audience you currently have.

When people share online they tend to do it for only a few reasons:

- They agree and want to look good by sharing it with their audience first
- They disagree and want to look good by sharing their counterpoint
- They find it helpful and want their audience to benefit from it as well
- They want to help support you by sharing your work with their audience

Whether it's shares, retweets, mentions, or any other form of sharing, this signal is the greatest opportunity to reach new audiences that you aren't able to with just your own reach.

Many creators can speak to a time where something they wrote went "viral", meaning that it spread to many more people than they could reach on their own.

My first experience was an article I wrote over a decade ago that went viral on Stumbleupon (if you remember that site or Digg.com, you've been at this as long as I have!), where a single post saw hundreds of views in a single night. For more than a decade that was the most successful post on my blog.

More often now, social media posts and content go viral because of algorithms. YouTube can put your video in front of a new audience. TikTok can share your work with millions of people that have never heard of you. A single retweet or even a like from a large Twitter account can help you reach tens of thousands of accounts that you wouldn't be able to reach otherwise, at least not for free.

Convert Signals into Ideas, and Ideas into Experiments

Once you start seeing any combination of these signals, you will start to see patterns—questions, struggles, ideas, obstacles—that the members of your audience share.

From there it's up to you to figure out which problems you want to solve—which "jobs to be done" you want to serve—and then come up with your own unique way of solving them.

May you take those signals and write a book, like I'm doing with this book right now.

Maybe you create an online course, or a resource in Notion, or an app, or a community of peers that provides accountability and connection. The product you create doesn't need to take thousands of dollars to create, or months and months of time in research and development.

Instead, you can put up a landing page and test the waters. Run a tiny, low-stakes experiment. I have done this with dozens of product ideas, many that have been left alone because the demand wasn't there.

For example, you can go to **build.craftsmancreative.co** to see one version of this. Rather than creating all of the course content and the community and the infrastructure, I put up a single landing page. I launched it to my email list and told the people who follow me on Twitter about it, and, to date, had 102 visitors to that page.

Now, the context around it is that it's a high-ticket group coaching program, which immediately rules out 90 percent-plus of my audience. But out of those 102 visitors, I only had one person sign up.

While that was an encouraging sign, it proved that there wasn't enough demand. My goal was to fill a beta group of ten people and then do quarterly launches of the program throughout 2022 with 25 spots open at a time. But if I can't get ten people or even two people, then how am I going to get 25?

The beauty of building products and creating projects this way is that there was no downside. I now know who my "true fans" are, and can serve them in the future when the audience has grown a bit more. I didn't spend any money creating the product first. I ran a free experiment in about two hours of my time and got a clear result.

When I ran a similar experiment for this book, I got a much different response. People started sharing, responding, emailing, DMing me, and all signs pointed to the fact that this was a "job to be done" for those interested readers.

So here I am, months later, writing chapters, hiring an editor, and preparing to self-publish a book in 2022.

Listen to your audience and let them tell you what they want you to make, and then go and make it in a way that only you can.

CHAPTER 23

Create Raving Fans by Treating Them as Customers

Mental models like this will help you make a decision once that serves you thousands of times in the future

As we get close to wrapping up this section on marketing, I want to leave you with two mindset shifts, sometimes called "mental models," to help you with the way you think about marketing. Mental models are shortcuts, often a single phrase that helps you make consistent decisions.

"Do unto others as you would have others do unto you" is a mental model. It can be used every time that you interact with someone. That's a shortcut, a mental model that will serve you throughout your entire life.

So, here's one more to end this section and segue into our next section, where we'll be diving into mastering sales.

Lead with value.

I love this because there are two ways you can take it. You can emphasize lead with value. Show up as a leader, charge forward and set the standard. That will help you attract followers as you set a vision for the future that you're working toward. It could also mean lead as in taking the first step. You act first, rather than wait to react to the way the people you meet choose to show up and interact with you.

The other is lead with value. That means that you have a mindset of service, of being helpful, of caring about other people's problems and helping them solve them. The more value that you can create early on, the more value will come to you in your life.

There's one caveat to this mental model. Lead with value happens even before any transaction has happened. This model isn't just for your clients and customers. It applies to everyone that you interact with—in life, at events, on social media, etc.

Lead with value. This mental model is how you create raving fans. People who talk about you unprompted. People who share your work, pay for everything you create, and can't wait for your next piece of content. Those raving fans are how you build your business. They're the foundation you build on when it comes to your audience, they help you define the culture, and help your business grow.

Treat them like your best clients even before any money changes hands, and they'll quickly see what it's like working with you. They'll want to become your clients because of how well you treated them in the early stages of the relationship.

You can use this mental model starting today. Think about how it can impact everyone you engage with—in person, on the phone or zoom, or online.

Lead with value, and the value will return to you with abundance.

PART 5

Sales Mastery

"You can have everything in life you want if you will just help enough other people get what they want."
— Zig Ziglar, Secrets of Closing the Sale

Sales was one area of my business I thought I had figured out, because when things got lean, I would go and "drum up some business" and come back with $120,000 or more worth of projects for the next six months. But then some of those projects would fall through, while others would get revised and the budgets would drop. Suddenly we'd end up with only $40,000 or $50,000 worth of work . . . for six months. When you have two business partners who are both 50/50 owners, that money doesn't stretch very far.

While I could go and sell when the time required it, I never set up a system to help me sell consistently, and I never realized how important it was to constantly be improving the clients I was working with. There's a massive difference between selling to someone who already wants what you're making, compared to trying to convince someone to buy from you who wasn't even considering it when you started your pitch.

That idea—the context that someone enters a buying decision with matters—is a huge lesson I wish I'd learned much earlier in my career as a creative. I also wish that I'd figured out how to extend my ability to sell to other areas of my business—from creative projects to financing movies, for example—and that I'd taken more seriously the importance of cash flow coming into the business in a high enough frequency to sustain the business.

In this section I'll share the lessons I've learned that have helped my business cross and stay above the six-figure mark, which are the same principles I'm using now to grow my business to a seven-figure, one person business over the next few years. When you take everything you've learned in the finance and marketing sections, combine it with your mastery of mindset, and add sales, you'll have a fully functioning business that's ready to be scaled in the next section using systems and frameworks for growth.

If you have any hesitancy around selling, I want you to know that we all feel that way at some point in our careers. But you no longer need to fear sales. Sales is service, and that mindset shift will help you grow your business into the sustainable, profitable, Craftsman-style creative business you deserve.

CHAPTER 24

The Journey from Marketing to Sales

Your business is like a highway . . .

Think about a road—a highway or an interstate. It stretches for miles and miles and gets people from point A to point B (and any number of other points) in the most direct way possible. Some people take detours, others prepare to do long stretches at a time with no stops.

Along the side of these roads are different places to stop called services—rest stops, overlooks and scenic views, pull offs in case you need to put chains on your tires or prevent an overheating engine.

You also have off ramps and onramps that can take you off the main road and into little towns, big towns, or in completely different directions altogether.

Once the roads existed, businesses saw opportunities to sell products, or "jobs to be done," to the people on the main road. Jobs like: My gas tank is getting close to empty; I need gas. I've been driving for too long, and it's getting late; I need a place to stay the night. The kids are hungry; we should get something to eat. So alongside the road you see billboards telling people "we can do that job!"

And some of the travelers pull off to get those jobs done.

Photo by Sean Foster / Unsplash

Your business is the same.

Marketing is like the interstate and its services. You put up a sign that says, "this road heads north," or "Los Angeles, 350 miles," and the people who want to go that direction or reach that specific destination will take your road to get there. There's no transaction. There's no cost other than their time and their choice to take your road over someone else's. So you can serve people by telling them that your road works better than other roads. "Six lane highway," "no tolls," or "scenic views." And the people who want to travel that way will hop on and start their journey.

Along the way, you provide even more value by providing the rest stops, the view areas, and the pull offs. Those come with the road; they're part of the marketing. They cost the traveler nothing.

An important point about this "marketing highway" is that you build the roads first. Only then do you add on the services. If you tried convincing people to come to your scenic overlook without a road to get there, you'd have a hard time getting any-one to come. But if you build the road first, it makes it that much easier for people to pull off and stop to take in the view.

You also wouldn't build a gas station out in the middle of nowhere! This "product" would fail miserably without the built in traffic that the highway provides. First, build roads. Once you have that traffic, that awareness, that interest, then you can learn from that traffic where to put different products and where to advertise them.

If cars keep running out of gas after one hundred miles on your highway, then they're showing you—very clearly—that they need a gas station before they reach that point. It would be a smart investment to put gas stations every thirty to fifty miles, and then put up billboards and signage letting people know that those gas stations exist.

If people keep crashing at night at mile marker 457, then you know that you should put a place for weary travelers to pull off and rest, or even make something nicer like a hotel or motel.

Build the roads first. Observe the behavior of the travelers that choose that road. Then add products and services to sup-port their journey.

None of this is "selling." It's providing the exact value that people need at the exact moment that they need it. The selling comes when people show up to your gas station, your restau-rant, or your hotel. They will have questions about how it works, the cost, and what they get in return. That's when you can sell to them, by helping them understand the value and how it will benefit them.

Sales in this scenario becomes easy—nearly effortless.

With this approach, we'll end this section on marketing, and move into more detail on sales—how you convert the traffic on your highway into customers that trust you to do the jobs that they need done.

CHAPTER 25

From Sales Funnel to Sales Journey

The success isn't in the funnel, the software, or the strategy. It's about giving your customer more context and value before they buy.

I've got a bit of a gripe I need to get out into the world.

I hate sales funnels.

I hate creating them. I hate being in them. I hate it when people talk about optimizing funnels. We've all been in one, and you likely know what it looks like and how it feels to be in a funnel: You sign up for a free webinar, or to download a free pdf or ebook. Then you get taken to another page with an instant upsell and then another after that. "Get my $499 course for only $47! You'll never get this discounted price again so you have to buy now!"

If you don't buy now, then your email is added to an email funnel where you're hit with a bajillion sales emails a day in and day out until you either buy or unsubscribe. Your affinity for the brand or creator is non-existent, you feel gross that you had to go through all that, and you'll never work with them again.

Sounds like an awesome way to bring new people into your business!

Okay, I digress.

Here's the principle for this chapter:

Say goodbye to sales funnels and replace them with sales journeys.

Sales Funnel Versus Sales Journey

A defining characteristic of sales funnels is that there is one way in and one way out. The goal of a business using a sales funnel strategy is to "dump" as many people into the top of the funnel so that they can get more people to come out the other end. You have to put in your email to get to the next part of the funnel, then you get hit with offers to buy, and more offers to buy, then, yes, more offers to buy. The hope is that 1 to 2 percent of people who enter the funnel come out the other side having purchased something from you.

Think about this from a broader perspective. While you might be happy converting one or two of every one hundred people, that means that there are ninety-eight to ninety-nine people who are turned off by your sales funnel approach and will never work with you again, despite at one point being interested enough to enter that sales funnel.

You just burned 98+ percent of people. That's the important thing to know about a sales funnel. And even if you can optimize that funnel to get to even 5, 8, or 10 percent conversion rate, you're still burning the relationship with 90 percent or more of the people who come in contact with you and your business.

The alternative, then, is a sales journey.

The Sales Journey

In a sales journey, you start by realizing that everyone is different, not only how they discover you and your business, but their level of interest at that moment, and their level of desire to learn more.

Not everyone who follows you wants to become a customer. They may just be interested in you, your journey, your story. Not everyone who subscribes to your email list is ready to purchase your product or service. Maybe they just want to get your newsletter each week or know when your next gig is.

If you treat everyone who comes into your world as if they're ready to buy—meaning that you instantly start selling to them—

many will turn around and leave. If instead, you meet them where they are in their journey and give them a lay of the land, they're much more likely to explore and one day become interested enough to become a customer.

Here's the principle:

Give without any expectation of a transaction, and leave the door open for those ready to take the next step.

The main difference is how you treat people. Do you greet them as a salesman or a guide? Treating people as a guide means that you can help them, rather than try and sell them. This mindset starts with those who aren't even following you yet. When you show up on Twitter or Instagram, find people who need help and serve them as if they're already a client or customer of yours. This gives them the experience of working with you and they start to see themselves as a customer. Often, they'll take that next step through the "open door" and subscribe to your email, message you directly, or otherwise.

Operating with a sales journey rather than a sales funnel means that you recognize that every single person is on their own path, with their own struggles, and their own desires. Rather than shove them through a one-size-fits-all funnel, open the door for them to take the next step.

Make it easy for people to become customers or clients, rather than forcing them through a funnel. Put a link in your bio. Put links in your weekly newsletter. Create free value for people and link to the things that would be the logical next step for someone in their situation.

Ask for Permission Before You Sell

The last point I'll make here is the importance of asking for permission before selling to people.

Your goal as a creative business owner is to serve people, to share your work with as many people as possible, not to optimize your conversion rate. (You'll do that, too, but it's not your main goal.) So rather than trying to sell everyone that enters your world, ask permission first.

The people who are ready will take you up on that offer and will let you sell to them. In that scenario, you'll have a much higher conversion rate than trying to sell to everyone.

In the fall of 2009, I had to take one of those . . . jobs. Ick. I hate even writing it. But times were tough, I had just married my beautiful bride, and we had a new life that I needed to help provide for.

So I got a job selling cars.

Yes. Me. Selling cars.

Funny enough, it's the only job I've ever been fired from, but that's a story for another time. Suffice it to say that being honest isn't always a desirable trait in that industry. The point of the story is that I learned a lot about selling in those four months. Rather than badgering every single person that came in the door, I spent much of my time researching and being certified in the three makes that we sold at the dealership: Porsche, Audi, and Volkswagen.

Within two months I was certified to sell all three, and those that had been there longer would come to me to ask questions about the different models on the lot. My service in that regard would earn me half of the commission on the sale, and I didn't have to do any of the negotiating or paperwork!

Within three months I was the second-highest earner at the dealership, and I was earning extra commissions directly from Audi for being certified. The sales that I did have came because I didn't lead with "what kind of car are you looking for today" when I greeted people on the lot. That presumed they were there to buy. Even back then, I knew better. Growing up my dad and I would often go to dealerships and test drive the coolest new cars, with no intention to buy whatsoever. So, instead, I asked how I could be helpful, or just sparked up a non-sales conversation.

While I would talk to fewer people in a given day or week, I would often sell a higher percentage of people, because I only tried to sell the people that signaled that they were interested. I wasn't trying to convince people; I was helping people get the car they came for at the best price.

Often, I'd even negotiate against myself to get people into a car that was a better fit. That's part of what got me fired . . . Needless to say, serving people first and only selling to those who want to be sold to is an incredibly powerful approach to doing sales for your business.

CHAPTER 26

Create an Irresistible, No-Brainer Offer

Selling this way is the most respectful way to sell to your audience

In this chapter we'll take all that we know about our audience, the signals that they've shown us in what jobs they want to hire us for, and then craft an offer — not just any offer, no. An irresistible, no-brainer offer. One where people respond with "take my money!"

When you build your audience, you observe what people resonate with content-wise. You pay attention to the requests people make of you and the things people want to hire you for.

As I was writing this book, I had inquiries for guest posts—people who wanted my writing. Invitations to come on podcasts—they wanted my voice and my stories. Requests for coaching—they wanted my strategy.

Once you have the signals, then you craft an offer that makes it easy for them to say, "Yes!" while also being something that you would enjoy doing and getting paid for.

The Qualities of a No-Brainer Offer

The easiest way that I've found to craft a no-brainer offer is to think in terms of investment and return.

Subscribing to a blog with your email is a very low investment, with potential high returns. That's why you can craft email signup pages that can get 10, 20, even 30 percent or higher signup rates. Meaning for every ten people that visit the page, three or more subscribe.

Master The Creator Economy Inline Form	109	29	26.61%
Master The Creator Economy Landing Page	344	51	14.83%

Two of my own signup forms for masterthecreatoreconomy. com

Once you start charging money, the investment increases, and so the return has to be much more tangible to the person purchasing your product or service.

Think of the last time you purchased a book. Did you have the thought of how much the ideas in that book might be worth to you? If you did, and that value was more than the cost of the book, you made the purchase.

Not all of us recognize that we make these emotional and logical decisions around purchasing, but it's what happens to everyone when they're faced with a decision to buy something. Emotionally, the product or service will either remove something painful from our lives or add something pleasurable.

Why do people buy expensive cars? They're terrible investments—the upkeep, the gas, the insurance, the monthly payments, the fact that it's a depreciating asset . . . the list goes on. Yet, Tesla has been the fastest growing car manufacturer over the last decade. Up until recently the cheapest car they sold was $65,000.

So, what gives?

People buy with emotion and justify with logic. For whatever reason, someone wants to drive a Tesla, so they buy the car. Then the logic side of the brain kicks in—the gas savings, it's better for the planet, the founder is inspiring, it has the fastest 0-60 time of any car . . . and on we go.

The same happens when someone is presented with an offer for your product or service. They will make the first yes/no decision emotionally, and then justify it with logic.

For example, buying a $2,000 course. What makes that course a "steal of a deal" or "way overpriced"? The emotional context that someone has when they see the price tag. Depending on their beliefs and their emotions, they'll make a fairly quick decision.

If, emotionally, they feel like $2,000 is a steal, they'll then start justifying that in their mind to make the purchase final.

This investment will return 10x when I implement everything in the course . . .

I get access to the course creator which is itself worth the price of admission . . .

Everyone else who has taken this course has grown their business . . .

And so on.

If, emotionally, they feel like it's overpriced, the logic kicks in to prevent them from buying it:

I could learn all this stuff for free on YouTube . . .

My buddy has the course, so I'll just ask to pay him a little bit for access (don't do this . . .) . . .

What I'm doing is working just fine, I don't need to spend that kind of money . . .

In order to make that price worth it I'd have to sell X number of Y . . .

This is just a scam for the course creator to get rich selling info, they don't actually know what they're talking about . . .

I've done both of these things just in the last month when it comes to buying courses, or crypto, or a new shirt, or food, or tickets to a show. Our initial yes/no decision is an emotional one, and then we justify it with logic. So, in order to create an irresistible, no-brainer offer, you first need to win over the emotional side of someone's brain, then appeal to their logic.

Emotional Selling

The first thing you need to do in your sales pitch or landing page is help someone have an emotional reaction. Help them see how their life would be better if they had what you're selling. Whether you're selling art, music, coaching, or an NFT, people need to feel how their life would be different with it—better than it is now.

In a potential customer, that feeling creates tension, which wants to be resolved or relieved (remember the spring sitting on my desk beside the dirty keyboard?). The only way they can relieve that tension is to buy your thing.

The rest of the offer pitch can appeal to their logic centers. Note: this movement into logical selling only works for people who have already decided to buy; the people who started with an emotional "no" have either left the page or checked out of the sales pitch already.

This step isn't about convincing people why they should buy; it's about reinforcing, logically, the decision they've already made to buy what you're selling. You can add more value by adding more and more and more for the same price. You've seen this before—"but wait, there's more," or "oh, and one more thing," or "buy one get one free." You expected to get X, but now you're getting X+Y! For the same price!

Another example is the way your offer is presented. Some photographers list their pricing directly on their website for anyone to see (and then comparison shop). Others will require that you inquire about a specific shoot and date before sharing their pricing. One photographer I've worked with, however, sees this exchange of information as an opportunity to differentiate his brand from everyone else. He creates personalized pricing pages on his website that are private to the couple or individual or business that is looking to hire him. He chooses the pictures, the verbiage, and delivers a one-of-a-kind page that makes the person viewing the page feel important and special. That this price is just for them. Rather than feeling the photographer is being secretive with his pricing, they now feel that this secret is shared between them, kept from the rest of the world. It changes the entire value proposition of that moment, and he's able to charge a premium because of how he makes people feel every step along the way from inquiry to the final delivery of their photos after the shoot.

Selling Isn't Just What Happens on the page

To tie all this back into the marketing efforts that led people to you, one of the most important things that will create the irresistible, no-brainer type offers for your business is the context people come with to your offer.

Meaning, what do they already know, think, believe, or feel before they've been presented with an offer?

If someone has been reading your tweets, subscribing to your email newsletter, and listening to your podcast for free for months, or even years, think of how much goodwill you've built up with them!

If the things you've taught them for free have had an impact on their life, imagine how they might think about your book, or your course, or your coaching?

If they enjoyed your music for "free" on Spotify and finally get the chance to come see you live in concert, imagine how much more fun they'll have singing along to their favorite songs of yours, compared to someone who's never heard you before. Which person is more likely to hit the merch table after the show?

The context matters and shouldn't be ignored when it comes to crafting offers.

So much of the success you have in selling depends on the context the potential customer or client has when they see or hear your offer. Imagine trying to sell an $85,000 car to someone who has never heard of your brand or your model before, compared to someone who has been a fan of Tesla for a decade and has been saving up that entire time to finally purchase that Model S. In the latter scenario you'll barely have to sell at all, because the context was set in the marketing over years, whereas with the customer who has never heard of your car before is starting from zero, and you've got to give them all this new context they need to emotionally be ready for such a long purchase.

I often tell creators that it's much easier to sell to people who already want what you're selling, than to convince people why they need to buy. There was a time where I went out to over two dozen venture capital firms in Utah to try and raise $400,000 to make an independent movie. I had in person meetings with about ten of them—the others turned me down prior to meeting with me—and in these meetings an interesting thing happened. I was told time and time again that my pitch was compelling, that they wished they could invest, but couldn't because their LPs— the Limited Partners, or investors in their fund—would be upset if they invested in a movie. Their whole fund was set up to invest in startups, or education, or health, or some other vertical, not entertainment or movies. I walked away from more than a month of meetings and hitting the pavement with $0 to show for it.

When I produced my first feature in 2021, it was a different story. The director had long-standing relationships with people who wanted to invest in her, and the other producer she brought in knew how to find grants and donations from other high net worth individuals and they nearly raised $1 million to make this movie in a matter of about two months.

The context that your potential buyer has before they are asked to buy something matters even more than your offer.

Putting It All Together

So, you know what people want to hire you for, you know what outcomes they want that they'll emotionally resonate with, you've supported that decision with logic, and have the proper context going into the offer..

How much do you charge?

This part is as important as any other step. And there's no clear-cut, one-size-fits-all answer. It depends. You can test it—try it at a price you think people will pay, then double it, then cut it in half, and see which one feels right.

Are you optimizing for more revenue, or more sales?

If you're a photographer, you'll certainly book more wedding gigs at $500 a pop compared to $5,000, but to make six figures a year you'd only need twenty at $5k, while you'd need two hundred at $500. I don't know any photographer who does two hundred weddings a year. Even twenty is a lot of work.

So how do you create an irresistible, no-brainer offer around your wedding photography packages? Utilize the three criteria we explored above (see how we're putting it all together?)

- Context - What do people think, feel, believe about you *before* they decide to hire you or check out your pricing page? That comes from your social media and your marketing.

- Value - How much are they getting compared to how much it costs?

- Logic - How can you support their decision to drop $5k for wedding photography with you?

One thing you can implement at the pricing stage is scarcity—taking control of the economics of the thing you're selling. If there are infinite amounts of the thing you sell, then the economics aren't in your favor. There's infinite supply, so demand will never be able to catch up. On the other hand, if you explicitly tell people that you only have twenty wedding slots for the year, and it's first come first serve, then you've limited the supply.

As long as you have more than twenty people who want to hire you, your price can go up.

It may not jump from $500 to $5,000 overnight, but you could increase your price every time you've sold three packages at the current price. So sell three at $500, then three at $1,000, then three at $1,500 and so on until you've hit $5k or even more!

Controlling the Amount of Supply Puts You in Control

You can tell your potential customers that you only have three coaching clients at a time, or can only take on two projects a month, or only do one speaking arrangement per month. That adds to the emotional decision-making process by creating the tension in the customer, who might think, "if I don't get this now, I may not get it at all."

It's not manipulative; it's just reality. You only have so much time, so you only want to work with people who are ready to buy from you right now. It's better for both of you in the long run.

Put this to the test—think about something you currently sell or want to sell. Put up a landing page, or send an email to a potential client, and implement everything covered in this chapter. Make sure you have the proper context before you present the offer. Then craft the offer in a way that makes it a no-brainer for them to say, "Yes!"

Here's a meta example for you. Over a period of months, I wrote this book in public and built a minimum (not quite) viable audience of a few hundred people. These new email subscribers wanted to receive new chapters by email when they read a chapter that was shared on social media or that one of their friends forwarded to them.

When I started editing the book along with my editor, I knew I needed to continue to build the audience and also start testing offers, so I put up an early access sales page which allowed the first 50 people to sign up to get a signed copy of the book, early access to the manuscript, a strategy call with me, and lock in pricing for the community all for $50 per year.

In the first week, I had five people sign up! While it's not a million-dollar launch, it proved that I had built up enough context with people that they saw the value in the offer. But here's what's interesting—three of the people who signed up were not already on the email list! These were people I had met and served on Twitter over the past few months, giving them feedback, chatting with them directly, and generally leading with value. I had built up enough context that when I presented an offer to get even more from me, they signed up immediately.

This method of selling respects the buyer by helping them make a quick decision one way or the other. If it's a yes, they feel good both logically and emotionally and they'll thank you for selling to them in that way. If it's a no, it's quick and easy, but they'll remember that respect in the future when their decision goes from a no, to a not yet, to a yes.

CHAPTER 27

The Sales Ladder

Create products and services at multiple price-points

The big mindset shift in this book is to think of yourself as a business owner, not just an artist or creator. One thing that sets businesses apart from individuals is that businesses have a suite of product and/or service offerings.

A graphic designer, for example, may only have one service offering—graphic design. But Adobe has a suite of products at various price points, and, not coincidentally, is valued at billions of dollars.

One thing we can learn from how big businesses operate is the idea that they have multiple products and/or services that can reach different people depending on where they are in their journey.

Apple may be the easiest example. You can use some of their products for free—Apple Music, Apple Podcasts, their Safari internet browser, and more. Then for just a few dollars a month you can subscribe to Apple music, or use their email and storage service iCloud, sign up for Apple TV+. For a few hundred dollars you can buy devices like an iPad, iPhone, or Apple TV. You can buy accessories like the AirPods or an Apple Pencil. For a few thousand dollars you can buy a laptop or desktop computer or buy their servers or other high-end systems. And you can invest hundreds of thousands, even millions, in their stock since they are a public company.

They have something for everyone, and truly understand the "job to be done" that these different products and offers satisfy for people.

Let's apply this to your creative business.

The Sales Ladder for Creators

The sales ladder looks a little like this:

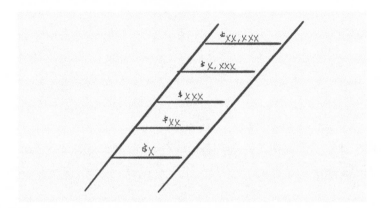

To start, before you even step up to the first rung of the ladder, you've got your free content, your marketing and social media profiles, and your email newsletter.

These are either free or can be had in exchange for entering one's email address in a form, like the one at the bottom right of the screen you're reading this on (unless you've already subscribed, in which case, thank you!)

Most creators make the mistake of skipping the first two rungs of the ladder and go straight for the third or fourth rung. They charge $XXX per hour or $X,XXX per project, which is great for when they can land that work, but they leave a lot of money on the table and make it harder for those "free" people to reach that next rung in the ladder.

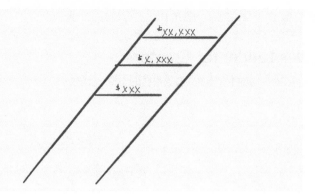

It just doesn't work very well.

The first and second rungs of the ladder are low-cost ways for people to go from follower or subscriber to customer. A $7 ebook. A $1.99 purchase of a song. A $3/month donation on **Patreon**. This changes the dynamic of the relationship, because now people aren't just receiving value for free, they're trusting you with an, albeit small, job to be done.

They become a customer.

Next is the second rung of the sales ladder, your $XX product offering. This could be a higher-priced ebook, a $20/month paid newsletter, a $49-99 course, a $29 webinar, the options are in-finite. Think of what you'd pay $10-99 to your favorite creators for. What "job" would you hire them for at that price?

Ask your existing audience what they would want for that price, or go into your messages and conversations with your au-dience to see what they've been asking you for that you could create and price on that second rung.

If you charge $10-99 per hour for your work you can put that on this rung as well, but realize that not every one of your follow-ers or subscribers needs to hire you as a client yet, so think about creating products at this rung, not just services. This will allow you to reach more people and convert them into customers.

The third rung you may already be familiar with. This is the bread and butter rung for most professional creatives who charge $100+ per hour for their time.

Photographers who charge $400 for a photo session. Musicians who get $250 a night for a gig. Filmmakers who get $300 a day for working on set. But this could also be a course that you charge more for—$129 or $249 or $495 or even $997. It could be a piece of art that you sell for hundreds of dollars. Having a good mix of services and products at this level will, by itself, help you create a six-figure business.

Most five-figure creators are working ten to twenty days a month and get around $400/day for their time. That works out to $48,000 to 96,000 per year. So you'd only need $4,000 to $52,000 worth of products on top of that service income to reach the six-figure mark.

A $199 product that you sell one per day of is $72,635. A $149 course, a $500 piece of art, an annual subscription to your newsletter or community for $100 a year.

It doesn't take much, and you can look at the gap between what you currently make and the $100,000 mark and divide by the $XXX price of your product to see how many you'd need to sell:

$100,000 - $75,000 = $25,000

$25,000 ÷ $129 = 193.78, or just under 200 courses, or webinars, or photographs, or graphic design packs, or anything else you want to create and sell for that price.

Up until 2019 all of my income was generated on the third rung of the ladder.

I charged $100 to $250 per hour for my time, depending on if I was producing, consulting, or who the client was. I was making just over six figures a year through 2018 and 2019. It wasn't until December of that year that I finally cracked the idea for Craftsman Creative and set out to build that product.

By the summer of 2020 I had produced half a dozen courses and crossed $15,000 in product income, of which I got 30 percent. So that new product income was bringing in over $1,500 a month and has grown since as I've added new courses each month. (We're now up to **16 courses** on the site!)

Since that time and learning the power of having products and services at multiple price points, I've added more and more to my own sales ladder. This book will ultimately be self-published and sold for $20, or likely ~$9 on Amazon (rungs 1-2). When I launch it, there will be a community for those who want to build six-figure businesses, which will start at $199 per year or $20/month (rungs 2-3). I also have a **consulting practice** where I come in as a "creative COO" for businesses trying to scale to seven figures, which I charge $X,XXX per month for, as well as **creative results coaching** for $1,000 per month.

Beyond that, my producing fees have moved from rungs 3-4 ($100 per hour or $1,000 per day) to a flat fee, which brings us to rung 5 of the ladder—the $XX,XXX offer for a product or service.

Now, as a percentage of my audience, there are only two or three people that hire me every year at that rung 5 price. If that's all I had, I would still have a six figure business. But, I'd be excluding everyone who wants to **work with me** at rungs 1-4 from ever becoming a customer or a client.

There's nothing inherently wrong with this approach, but it can take a decade or more to get to the point where you can charge $XX,XXX for a project.

So the way to build a resilient, diversified six-figure creative business is to look at the sales ladder and try to create a product or service that satisfies the "jobs to be done" of your audience at each level.

Create a free entry point like a newsletter or free community. Then create products in the $X and $XX ranges. Add products as well as services at the $XXX rung 3 level. And expand up to include people who want to hire you for $X,XXX and $XX,XXX jobs.

Don't just limit yourself to one rung or think that you can't ever reach rungs 4 or 5. You may only get one or two people per year hiring you at that level, but as your audience grows and evolves, more and more people will become customers and more will want to work with you at those higher levels.

CHAPTER 28

Create More Value Than Anyone Else

Don't hold yourself back with fear of being too "salesy"

For some reason, many creatives hesitate to "do sales" because of the fear of being "too salesy" with their audience. I want to help you get over your fear and hesitation, and reframe what sales is so that you can sell more and provide more value to the audience you seek to serve.

Sales is service.

Take a step back from the verbiage, the pricing, the offer, and the need that your business has to generate revenue through sales. Think about the way you've built your business up to this point through the different chapters in this book.

You've come up with an amazing vision for yourself and your business that drives you to serve a group of people every day.

You've spent time, sometimes months or even years, to find an audience of people. Not so that you can grow some arbitrary number of followers or subscribers, but so that you can serve them.

You discovered their pain points and their needs and desires, listened to them, observed where you can be of service.

You then took the time and had the faith to create a product or service with no guarantee that it would work, but you pushed forward, willing to tweak and optimize it so that it did the job that your audience needed to get done.

Now, imagine that after all of that work, you connect with someone in your audience who desperately needs this thing you make . . . And you don't give them a chance to buy it. That's what you're doing when you avoid selling your product or service. You rob people of the opportunity of getting their needs met, or hiring you for that job they need done.

Why would you do that?

Fear. Fear that you'll fail. That you'll let them down. That you're not good enough.

But I'd invite you, again, to think about everything you've done up to this point to be the person that people come to for this job. They trust you. They like you. They want to hire you!

In this context, selling that person isn't gross! It's service! You're giving them exactly what they came here for, the exact thing you promised in your marketing. You've already created a ton of value. Now it's time to give it to people.

Now, if the only reason you're selling things to people is to make money, then we've got a different problem here. Your issue isn't fear of failure or that you're not good enough—it's fear that you'll be found out.

If you find yourself in that situation, simply just shift your approach to be one of service then of extracting dollars from a group of people.

Create More Value Than Anyone Else

The way you do this is by creating more value that exceeds the dollar amount that you've decided to put on your product or service.

Rather than thinking about how you can get more profit by charging more, think about how you can create more value that's worth more money so that it's easy to charge more. It's a subtle shift, but it puts your focus on the value you're creating rather than the dollars you're getting.

Think of the job or jobs that people are hiring you to solve. What could you do that no one else is doing to provide more value? A personal touch, an unexpected bonus, a better product than anyone else is creating?

You can survey the landscape of your industry and your market and see what everyone else is doing. While discounting your price to be the most affordable is one form of value creation, that's not what will be of most service to your audience.

How can you go above and beyond, so that even if you're the most expensive option, you offer more value than anyone else can so that people aren't deciding to hire you based on price, but based on your offer and the value you've created?

When I produced my first feature film in the spring of 2021, I was asked to be the line producer—the person who decides how to spend the money and manages that spend throughout the production—as well as the Unit Production Manager or UPM— the person responsible for hiring the crew, dealing with any issues, and ensuring that everyone gets taken care of.

For most productions those are two separate, full-time jobs. But I knew that the film's budget wasn't enough to hire both, so I offered to do both jobs. On top of that, I did all of the production accounting during preproduction, production, and post.

Now, while I made more money than I would have doing just one job, I also provided more value than any other producer could in that moment because I knew I could do the jobs and that it would be extremely valuable to the production.

While I may not do that again (three full time jobs is a bit extreme), it was my foot in the door to the industry I'd been trying to break into as a producer for over a decade. That value led to more offers to produce, at a higher fee, because I set myself apart as someone who is going to create more value for a production than anyone else, despite what I get paid to do so.

You can do the same for your audience and the people hiring you for their jobs to be done. Go the extra mile, treat them like a six-figure client even if they only purchased a $10 album.

Send hand-written thank you notes, do more work than was expected, connect people with others, teach what you know, share the behind the scenes, insider secrets that are hard to find when you're trying to enter a creative field. Create and give more value than anyone else, and the magical thing that happens is that more opportunities, money, connections, and success comes back to you.

Just as you need to exhale in order to inhale, the more you give, the more you receive. Approach your work with the commitment to creating more value than anyone else.

CHAPTER 29

Maximize Lifetime Value by Creating Happy Customers

Shift what you optimize for in your business, and everything changes

This chapter presents one of the most important sales mindset shifts you can make as a creator. The goal of selling isn't just to make sales, increase revenue, etc. If you're not including the goal of creating happy customers, you risk minimizing the long-term value of each customer.

Credit where credit is due, this idea came from the work of André Chaperon and Shawn Twing from **Tiny Little Businesses**. Their entire company exists to help creators learn email marketing, traffic generation, and how to create these happy customers. If you want to **read the inspiration for this chapter**, I promise you won't be disappointed, as their writing is my favorite on the internet. I can't wait for their email newsletter every week. Heck, I can't wait for them to sell me something because every time they do, they deliver a week's worth of value-packed emails before presenting their offer. They have mastered the craft of creating happy customers, and it's one of the best things I've learned from them. I'd be holding out on you if I didn't share it with you here.

Create Happy Customers

Here's a quote and statistic that the guys at TLB have shared a number of times over the last few years:

Legendary marketer Dean Jackson has analyzed his customers' extensive data and found that only 15% of people who buy within two years make a purchase in the first 90 days. Everyone else — 85% of people who buy — don't make a purchase until AFTER 90 days. That means there's FOUR TIMES THE OPPORTUNITY waiting for you after three months — if, and only IF, you don't screw it up.

Think of everything we've covered about sales—connecting the journey from marketing to sales, abandoning the funnel and replacing it with the sales journey, creating irresistible offers and a ton of value. All of it is because of this reality stated in the quote above.

Most people don't buy in the first ninety days, let alone the first contact with an offer. Yet, so many people today push the sales funnel approach. Dump people in at the top, squeeze as many people through the bottom as possible.

But that approach ignores this reality completely.

You're burning most of the people that you "dump" into that funnel, and they'll never return. You'll never have the chance to sell to them in ninety days, let alone a year from now, if you turn them off on first contact.

You're creating upset visitors rather than happy customers.

So it's time to flip the script and use a different approach. Focus, instead, on creating happy customers.

Here are the principles of creating happy customers.

Let Them Choose How and When to Discover Your Offers

Remove the funnel, the countdown timer, the urgency of the offer initially. You haven't yet earned their trust, so it just feels icky on first contact. Those tactics can sometimes work in the future around Black Friday or Cyber Monday, product launches, or other times. But if that's how people are discovering your brand and your offer, it's often more of a turnoff than a reason to buy now.

Instead, provide a ton of value upfront and open the door for people to enter your world by giving you their email address. This will give you the permission to give them more value over time.

When I launched my courses in the spring of 2020, the very first person to pay full price was a guy that had been on my email list for over four years.

Four years of value! Email newsletters, free email series, webinars, and videos that I shared for four years. That subscriber had the opportunity to go at his own pace and choose when to become a customer because my business was set up to create happy customers, rather than quick-as-possible ones.

Don't Use Email to Just Sell

Too many creators and businesses, especially, use email as a way to deliver promotions to inboxes. It's a limited view of what that relationship can be.

Can you believe that there are emails that I look forward to receiving every week? Well, there are. Two of them. The first I already mentioned, from **Tiny Little Businesses**. The other comes less consistently, but any time Derek Sivers sends an email I know that there's some value on the other end.

Every time Derek announced another book, I bought it. Every time this year that TLB has launched another course, I've bought it. They've provided so much value for free, for years, that I know how much value must be in a paid product or service.

You could easily say I'm a happy customer since I own every one of both of these creators' products.

Have a Long-Term Approach to Your Business

I know that the work I'm doing right now isn't going to pay off next week or next month. But I also know that when it does start paying off that it won't be for just a week or a month.

This book I'm writing will be a calling card and an entry point for future happy customers for years to come. The movies that

I produce will, hopefully, impact audiences for many years. Generations, if I'm lucky.

When you approach your creative work this way, it means that every new creation compounds on the ones you've already created. It creates a whole library of assets that you own that people can buy on their own timeline. It's one of the reasons that I don't love the current craze over cohort-based courses. The value is limited to a small group of people for a limited amount of time.

In order to reach more people, you have to show up over and over again as a creator, which limits your freedom and independence. Those assets are only assets during the short period you promote and run the course. After that, since people missed the window, the value is gone.

The alternative is to create a whole bunch of assets that can be purchased by anyone at any time, whether they just discovered you or have been a fan for years.

You Treat People Differently Depending on What Your Goal Is

If your goal is to extract as much money from an audience in as short a period as possible, you are going to treat people like numbers. You won't care about their experience, only about how to get money from their bank account into yours.

You care less about the quality of your product, but about how many you can sell. You don't care if they don't come back later, because there are a million others you can put that offer in front of next. This approach feels exhausting to me, not to mention gross and disrespectful.

When you optimize for happy customers, you put more care into your product. You consider how to get those customers to share your work with others, to leave glowing reviews, and to want to connect with you, the creator.

You give them options rather than force them through a funnel.

You provide value indefinitely because that's how you operate and then leave the door open for those fans and subscribers to take the next step and become customers when they feel that they're ready.

Your business completely changes when you change what you're optimizing for.

CHAPTER 30

Sell to Your Audience Directly at the Start

Sell directly to your audience at first.

One last chapter on sales to help as you get started with this new approach and framework.

You've done the work to build an audience of people you want to serve with your products and services, and now it's time to sell to them. Artists will often look at different platforms like Amazon, Apple Music or Spotify, or others to sell their products, or Product Hunt or other directories to launch their businesses.

While these platforms can help boost awareness and get more people into your world, they rarely will give you the desired outcomes of a sustainable business because the people you connect with there aren't yet part of your audience. They lack the context, so they are even less likely to buy than your existing audience.

And by sending your existing audience over to some platform, you're giving up a ton of the financial upside. The Apple App Store takes 30 percent of revenue, the Kindle store takes 30 to 35 percent, even Kickstarter takes 5 percent, Patreon 8 percent, and who knows with Spotify.

At the beginning, when your audience numbers in the hundreds or even thousands, sell directly to your audience. Send them a link to a sales page that you control, or even just have them send you money directly.

How to Sell Directly to Your Audience

There are two creator-friendly companies that have built tools for creators to sell directly to their audience. I've used both successfully. I've invested in these companies and have used them since their first year in business.

ConvertKit is a marketing platform for creators. You can build an email list, create and sell products, even set up a tip jar! Their email marketing software is my favorite and what I recommend to every creator who wants to use email as part of their marketing strategy. I've set up my coaching payments through Convert-Kit, as well as a virtual tip jar for my Web 3 for Creators post.

Craftsman Creative Results Coaching

Weekly coaching to help creatives produce the outcomes that matter to them and their businesses.

We start with creating a map of where you are, where you're going, and how you want to get there, then work together toward that specific outcome.

Pay month to month, or save by paying yearly.

Monthly	Yearly
$1000.00	$10000.00

Get Started

Coaching Sales Page

🫙 Web3 For Creators - Tips   ○○○

1 TIP • $10.00

Virtual Tip Jar

The other platform that I've used successfully is **Gumroad**. They are similar to ConvertKit in that they are a marketing and sales platform, but their emphasis is more on the sales side, where ConvertKit's focus is more on the email marketing side. You can quickly create a product and launch your own sales page inside Gumroad, add affiliate links and payouts, and add multiple price tiers and offer discounts.

My first book, The Indie Film Sound Guide

You can even offer a "pay what you want" price, as in the image above.

Products are a bit more robust on Gumroad, but if you're going the email marketing route, you won't be disappointed in ConvertKit. (Note that Gumroad just changed its pricing so that there is a percentage involved in **selling on their platform**.)

You can head directly to either of these platforms and set up an account and create your first sales page in less than thirty minutes. Then, rather than sending people to Spotify or Amazon or some other big platform, you become the platform!

You don't pay ridiculous fees, you don't have to wait for the platform to pay you the money you've made, and you can have a direct connection with your audience. The biggest reason to sell directly to your audience is that when people buy from you, you get their email addresses!

You have no idea who has purchased your product on Amazon, or who has listened to your music on Spotify. They don't share the info of the people who are buying what you're selling, so it prohibits you from growing your audience in that way.

With ConvertKit or Gumroad, you know every single person that has chosen to become a subscriber as well as a customer, so you can have a more direct relationship to them, and your audience grows with each new purchase.

Extend Distribution Through Platforms

Once you reach a certain point in your business and with your sales, you can then strategically use these other platforms for distribution.

The risk of relying on these platforms too early is the same as building your audience on these platforms. YouTube could remove a bunch of your subscribers. Facebook could increase the cost to reach your audience. Twitter can de-platform you by canceling your account.

The same goes for these other platforms. They could change their payment structure, lock you out of your account, or refuse to pay out the money you've earned. Until you have a reliable amount of money and growth happening on your own without these platforms, you should focus there first. Then, strategically use these platforms to get more sales. Not all of the sales, just more of them.

List your book on Amazon after you've sold the first few hundred copies to your audience in a presale. Put your music up on Apple and Spotify after you've given your audience a link to purchase the music directly from you first. Put your product up on Etsy after you've sold it to your audience on your own Shopify store.

Making this shift in the way you sell rewards the trust and permission that your existing audience has already given you. You can give them early access, discounted pricing, or one-of-a-kind versions of your work because they're part of your inner circle, not just some random person who saw an ad and bought your thing on a whim.

Your audience wants that special attention and access to you. So give it to them!

The platforms will always be there ready to make money off of you. Make money for yourself first by selling directly to your audience.

PART 6

Leverage, Systems, Growth Mastery

"It is much easier to put existing resources to better use, than to develop resources where they do not exist."
— George Soros

We've made it. Moving from a humble Contractor to an experienced Craftsman with a new mindset and a new approach to running your business, you've done the work to learn and apply the principles in this book. But you're not done.

There is another step to take once you've built your new business. If you remember all the way back to the parable at the start of the book, there was one huge difference between how I ran my business as a contractor and how I run it now as a craftsman.

Leverage.

Understanding leverage took time, but it has been one of the most rewarding parts of this whole journey, and it can be for you, too. I started reading about leverage, and then later systems thinking and mental models and principles and frameworks, around the middle of 2018. Naval Ravikant was someone I was introduced to through the Tim Ferriss podcast, and he wrote a—now quite famous—Twitter thread that starts, "How to get rich (without getting lucky):"

In it he talks about different kinds of leverage—capital, people, and products (code and media). It was then that I realized the leverage I had. I knew how to create media, arguably better than most that I would consider my competitors. I understood the story. I knew all the aspects of the craft of creating video and audio media. I began to see a different path ahead.

At the time it truly felt like a fork in the road. I could keep going down the road I was on and end up like so many others who had taken that path—trading time for dollars until the day I was able to finally retire without enough to show for it all at that matter.

While unclear I was unclear where the other path would lead me, and though it had potentially rougher terrain, it had a pull to it. Something intangible was enticing me to leave the safer path and venture into the unknown. Yet it didn't feel scary. I knew that I had the tools and resources I needed to survive anything, and that this was the path I wanted to take.

As I write this, years later, I know that it was the right decision. I have begun to see the power of leverage, what can be done with a group of people aligned toward a singular goal (making a movie), the kind of leverage that content creates (courses and blog posts and email newsletter and books), and I'm starting to see the potential that capital can have to move markets and change lives. I started Craftsman Creative as a way to leverage my skills in producing video at the start of the pandemic, but it took off when I began to invest my capital, both my money and my time, into other creators to help them create courses at no out-of-pocket cost.

The results spoke for themselves. Within the first year we crossed $50,000 in sales, two creators added five-figures of additional revenue to their businesses from just a few days' work, and the company grew month over month, even when I wasn't able to work on it while I was producing a movie in the spring of 2021. I spent the rest of 2021 building systems and creating even more leverage so that the business can grow even more in the years to come, so that I have even more profit to reinvest in other creators, so that I can contribute to the lives of even more creators and make an impact in the creative industries that I love.

I started this book focused on money, revenue, debt and all the things that I didn't have enough of. But my mindset has changed. I'm now focused more on gratitude and contribution. What matters more to me now than the amount of dollars I make—either annually or hourly—is the size of the impact I can have by implementing this leverage and understanding my business more and more every day.

That's what this last section is about. I want to help you see that it's not just about going from a five-figure creator to a six-figure business owner. It's about fully leaving the Contractor's mindset behind for the Creator's. To care about the craft, yes, but to care more about the legacy you want to leave, the change you want to make in the world, and the way you want to impact the lives of those around you.

CHAPTER 31

Systems Thinking for Creatives

It's all connected

This topic has been a rabbit hole for me for a few years now.

The idea originally surfaced when I read Thinking in Systems by Donella Meadows. It's a transformational book that I believe Seth Godin or André Chaperon recommended a few years ago.

Since then I've read other books and blogs and watched videos about systems thinking. I now feel that this concept is one of the most powerful principles I can share with those I get the chance to work with.

By the end of this chapter, you'll see your business in a whole new way, I hope. By embracing system's thinking, you can change your approach to growing your business and see results like you've never had before. Once you understand how to see your business as a system, you'll never be able to go back.

Defining A System

From Thinking in Systems:

> *A system is a set of things—people, cells, molecules,*
> *or whatever—interconnected*
> *in such a way that they produce their own pattern*
> *of behavior over time.*

In this book, we've covered different parts of your business—finances, marketing, audience building, sales, offers, and your mindset as the business owner. It would be easy to see them as separate, independent parts. For example, if you want to grow your audience more, focus on growing your audience.

In reality, these different parts of your business are interconnected. Any change or improvement to one part affects the other connected parts of your business. When you improve your offer, your audience grows, which impacts your sales and revenue and helps you see yourself as a successful business owner. These different parts of your business aren't siloed. They are interconnected, and that interconnectedness is what produces outcomes.

The shift to make is one of linear to non-linear thinking. Rather than marketing > audience > offer > sales > revenue, a linear view of your business and its different parts looks more like this:

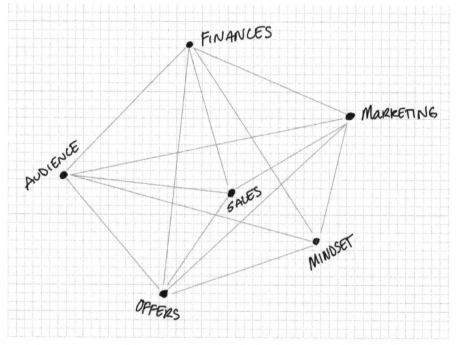

Every part of your business connects and relates to the other parts. It's not a line, but a multi-dimensional, sector-dependent shape. Boy, I wish I knew that years ago . . .

The Problem with Linear Thinking

When I ran a video production company, linear thinking was arguably my greatest failure. I wrongfully thought that every part of the business would operate in its own "box." If money was tight, I would go and book more work to fix the "revenue" box. If we had too much work, I would jump in and help with the editing. When those projects were done, I'd go and find more.

It was a very reactionary way of operating, one born from our over emphasis on siloing things, keeping them separate in essence, and it served us poorly. The failure to see the business as a system rather than just a "sum of its parts" led to burnout and nearly bankrupted us.

I would book $100k worth of projects at the beginning of the year. Then we would rush to service all those clients, often missing deadlines or having a project fall through. That $100k would turn into only $30 to 40k worth of revenue, which was only enough for two to three months.

But because we'd booked the work, I was too busy helping in post-production to go out and find new work. So that two to three months of revenue would have to stretch to four, five, even six. And then if a client didn't pay on time, we were really hosed.

As soon as I was free to go get more work, I'd go and book a bunch of new clients, but those new clients wouldn't start for weeks or months, which means the money from those projects wasn't coming any time soon either.

Outside of all this, I wasn't paying enough attention to my business partner and what he was going through.

This linear thinking and reactionary way of running a business ended in me going $15k in debt to try and keep the business afloat—another linear decision. We were out of money, we needed to float a month or two of payroll before our next projects came in, so I took on debt to pay our salaries. But then, those projects never panned out. We found ourselves at the end of the year with no clients, no projects, no revenue, and no business.

I left that business in 2017 and vowed to figure out what went wrong so I never repeated it again.

Fast forward four years and systems thinking is one thing that could have saved us, had I known how to operate with that framework back then.

Optimizing Linearly Can Hurt Your Business

Linear thinking isn't just dangerous to a business. It can be deadly. It was for my company.

Let's return to sales funnels for more proof. Most people would agree that getting more people through a sales funnel is good for a business. So they optimize that funnel for a singular outcome—more customers. However, because of their linear thinking, they end up hurting the business.

More customers aren't always good. If you acquire your new customers at a loss, then hope to make an upsell to a percentage of the new customers your funnel generates, more customers could actually mean more expenses. How long can you sustain a loss? If you have shipping involved with your business but are acquiring a lot of small sale customers, you might lose money from the shipping, or from paying for returns.

More of the right customers, happy customers, on the other hand, is what businesses need to optimize for. To do so, you have to understand the relationship between your marketing, your offer, your sales, and your audience. Only then can you attract the right people, people who can afford what you're selling as well as see the value in it.

That approach busts the limits of linearity and takes into account how all the different parts of your business support each other.

Had I done this with my last business, I would have never stopped finding new clients. I would have created a system to generate new leads and new projects every week, because if the projects stop coming in, so does the revenue. Had I known that our mindset as business partners was so essential to the success of the business, I would have set aside more time for conversation and rest so that we didn't get burnt out. I never would have taken on debt but would have found other ways to optimize the business to be profitable and more sustainable.

But those actions require a different perspective.

The Emergent Quality of a System

A system is a set of inputs and outputs that, when operating properly, creates an outcome. A simple example is a bathtub. You've got water from a faucet pouring into a tub, and a drain that allows that water to run out of the tub. You can add more parts, like a temperature knob to control the temperature of the water. You could use a thicker or different material for the tub so that the water inside holds its temperature for longer. You can improve the stopper in the drain so that less water leaks out. When all of these parts work together as an optimized system, the emergent quality is a nice hot bath that lasts for a long time.

To start thinking in systems for your business, you need two things:

1. An understanding of the emergent qualities your system should create

2. An understanding of the different parts of your system and their relationship to each other

When you start to see your business this way, you start thinking more like a business owner than a creator with a lot of different jobs. You can spend time working on your business, rather than in your business. You can optimize the system to get the emergent qualities that you care about, whether that's happy customers, more revenue, more freedom and independence, or more impact.

In a previous chapter, I talked about creating "happy customers." That's the emergent quality I want for my businesses. I know that if happy customers are emerging from the system that is my business, then the system is operating how I want it to.

If, on the other hand, I'm getting a lot of mean or confusing comments in response to my work, or not seeing any sales of my products, or my audience isn't growing, or my revenue isn't growing, then I know that the system isn't working properly.

Since the emergent quality isn't present, I can dive into the system and experiment to see which part I need to focus on in order to fix things (i.e., have that emergent quality appear).

Don't just run from fire to fire in your business, addressing things when it's too late. Take a step back, see your business as the system that it is, learn to understand the relationships between the different parts, then ask yourself how you can tweak and optimize the system to be better at generating the outcomes that you care about most.

CHAPTER 32

Theory of Constraints

Your ability to identify the constraints in your business is what will unlock your ability to grow.

In one of my favorite reads from the last few years, *The Goal*, by Eliyahu Goldratt, the author tells a narrative story that teaches a profound principle.

He calls it the "Theory of Constraints."

In the story, a team must solve the problems in their manufacturing plant before the plant gets shut down. They've been given three months to turn things around. They take a different approach to not only stop the bleeding of cash but ultimately become the most profitable location in the company. The way they did it was through the theory of constraints.

By the end of this chapter, you'll learn to be more productive and effective in the way you run your new creative business through the application of this principle.

Productivity, Goals, and Measurements

The book starts by defining productivity in a highlight that I've bolded, underlined, and highlighted in my notes:

> **Productivity is the act of bringing a company closer to its goal. Every action that brings a company closer to its goal is productive. Every action that does not bring a company closer to its goal is not productive.**

With this definition, productivity is meaningless unless you know what your goal is. This is, in part, why this book started with your vision, purpose, and goals.

Let's take a goal that we introduced early in the book as an example—to become profitable from the start. To determine if you're moving closer to or further away from that goal—if you're being productive or not—you measure three parts of your business:

1. Throughput
2. Inventory
3. Operating Expense

Throughput is the rate at which your system (your business) generates money through sales. Inventory is all the money that you've invested in purchasing things that you intend to sell. Operational expense is all the money your business spends to turn inventory into throughput.

The goal, using these definitions, is to increase throughput while simultaneously reducing both inventory and operating expense. Said differently: sell more while spending less. To move closer to your goal in the most efficient way possible, you use the Five Focusing Steps:

1. IDENTIFY the system's constraint.
2. Decide how to EXPLOIT the system's constraint.
3. SUBORDINATE everything else to the above decisions.
4. ELEVATE the system's constraint.
5. If in the previous steps a constraint has been broken Go back to step 1, but do not allow inertia to cause a system constraint.

But to do that, we need to understand what a constraint is.

Identifying the Constraints in Your Business

Broadly speaking, you can see which of the three areas is holding you back from being more productive. If you aren't selling enough products or services, the constraint may be with your throughput. If you constantly run out of inventory or can't deliver more product or serve more clients, then your constraint would be with your inventory. If you don't have enough capital to buy inventory or pay your team or run ads, you've got an operational expense problem.

Since you're a creative business owner and not the manager of a manufacturing plant, your constraints are going to be different. You're creating art. You're serving clients. There's likely just you. So how do you take these five steps and identify the constraints in your business?

Let's look at my old video production company as an example.

My system wasn't working. I was trying to optimize each part of the business without understanding the relationship it had, or the theory of constraints. I had constraints in two of these areas—we didn't have enough clients or projects (throughput), and we didn't have enough capital to invest in the business (operational expense). Had I understood and spent time identifying the greatest constraint in my business, I would have focused on throughput.

Here's why: Without enough demand, you could have infinite money and infinite supply, and still no profit.

Look at another example—Quibi. It was founded by some big names in the film industry at the end of 2018, raised $1.75 billion dollars, launched at the start of the pandemic in April 2020, and then shut down in December of 2020, eight months later, because they didn't have enough subscribers. It was sold earlier this year to Roku for a mere $100 million dollars.

You could raise all the money in the world and still not have enough demand for your product. Quibi's issue wasn't one of inventory or operational expense; it was one of throughput.

My production company suffered the same fate. Even after taking on debt to fix the operational expense problem, we still had a massive throughput constraint. We didn't have enough demand.

If you want to be profitable from the start, you need to create a situation where you always have more demand for what you sell than you can supply.

If five people want to hire you for coaching, offer four slots.

Rather than simply putting your music on Spotify and Apple (unlimited supply), create one hundred signed physical albums and sell them to your superfans for $50. As long as you have more than one hundred people who want to buy them, you'll sell out.

I currently can only take on three feature film projects a year, because each one takes about 3.5 months to produce. I don't want to work twelve months a year with no breaks, so I only have three slots available.

If more than three people want to hire me, I'll stay busy, and I'll raise my rates with every new project. Had I known this theory back then, I would have built a system that consistently delivered three to five new leads every week, people that were potentially interested in hiring us for video production services. At first the system would have been manual, but I would have figured out how to outsource and automate it until it was working in the background.

With three to five new leads, I knew I would land one new client a week, and our client projects ranged from $10,000 to $20,000 each. That would have been plenty to keep us in business, and likely would have helped us grow the business and expand the team. How do I know this would work? Because I built this automated system for Craftsman Creative.

It started as a manual process— reaching out to influencers and creators directly online. Once I figured out the script that worked best, I hired a person on Upwork for $100 a week to find me the emails of twenty or more creators each week. She then puts those emails into a spreadsheet, which automatically pushes those emails to PersistIQ and emails them four prewritten emails over three weeks.

If they respond, it goes to my email, and I can follow up. If not, they are taken off the list never to be bothered again. This process gets me one to two calls a week with new course creators, and I have an 85 percent close rate on those calls. (I actually had to turn the system off for the month of December 2021 because

I was too far out with the courses that I'd already booked! The system was working too well.)

You can take the same approach to the other two constraints around inventory and operational expenses. Following the five-step process, you start by identifying the constraint in your business. You can start broad—we have an inventory constraint, there's not enough parts coming from overseas—and then narrow down.

Once you've identified the constraint, you follow the next steps to exploit, subordinate, and elevate in order to remove the constraint. Then you start over by identifying the next constraint in your business. Doing this process all but guarantees that you'll grow your business. It works that well.

Maybe your greatest constraint is lack of awareness, or sales, or the offer. Any of the chapters in this book could shine a light on a constraint in your business. Using the theory of constraints, you are now empowered to go identify the constraints in your business and take action to improve your business.

CHAPTER 33

Planning Your Life for Inevitable Success

Taking your work seriously and protecting your time are important habits to build.

When I started writing this book, I turned to my wife and said, "regardless of how many books I sell, how many new subscribers I get, or how many people read the words I write, if nothing changes in their life, then I'll feel like I failed."

I meant what I said. I've done everything I can to put actionable principles down on paper in hopes that you'll be inspired to try anything that I've covered in this book in your own life and business.

This chapter has been one of the most transformational in my day-to-day life. It helped me write this book in just over three months while prepping a feature film, producing a short film and a music video, and planning out a content strategy for Craftsman Creative for 2022. Not to mention producing four seasons of television, starting two businesses, strengthening my marriage and my relationship with my three boys, and starting a consulting practice all in the last three years.

I don't list out these accomplishments to seem impressive, but to impress upon you how powerful the principles in this chapter are.

In one way we're talking about time management, but the scope is much bigger than that. This is about bridging the gap between knowledge and action. It's about owning that you're responsible for the outcomes in your life and your business. It's about raising your standards and taking massive action to create the life and business you've always wanted.

I want to share five thoughts from a mentor of mine—Tony Robbins, who I've mentioned before and been able to spend some time with—along with some thoughts of my own.

One reason so few of us achieve what we truly want is that we never direct our focus; we never concentrate our power. Most people dabble their way through life, never deciding to master anything in particular.

This idea is so empowering if you have the right attitude. You could take offense, or you could step up to the plate. Choose to focus, to concentrate, to master your life. This is the first decision—to choose mastery. Choose to raise your standards. Choose to be different and to do more than anyone else.

If you talk about it, it's a dream. If you envision it, it's possible. If you schedule it, it's real.

This is a more tactical thought, and below I'll cover the RPM system that Tony teaches to plan out your projects, your year, months, weeks, and days, and help you see the right next step to take at all times.

Deciding to commit yourself to long-term results rather than short-term fixes is as important as any decision you'll make in your lifetime.

You'll notice in this book that I have never promised quick results. The main reason for this is because I haven't experienced them myself in my career. There have been times that I've immediately seen the difference in a new approach, but the results often lag for months or even years.

The goal I had to produce a feature film took twelve years! I attribute a ton of the achievement of that goal to this principle of being committed to long-term results rather than short-term tactics or hacks. It's served me well and I can't wait to see the results that come in years and decades from the decision to write this book.

Once you have mastered time, you will understand how true it is that most people overestimate what they can accomplish in a year— and underestimate what they can achieve in a decade!

This expands our vision to include a much longer timeline. What do you want your life to look like next year, but also in five or ten years?

What do you want to accomplish? Who do you want to become?

Go back and read your vision from the first part of the book and see what you're now inspired to add or change with this new perspective.

People who succeed at the highest level are not lucky; they are doing something differently than everyone else.

This was the key insight that changed my trajectory over the last two years. I realized that there were people who were operating at a different level than I was. They were achieving more, making more, connecting more, had more opportunities, and had a different approach to the way they lived their lives.

I was inspired by people like Tony Robbins, Seth Godin, Derek Sivers, Brene Brown, Barack Obama, Brian Clark, Steven Pressfield, Jim Collins, Sahil Lavingia, Steve Martin, Shonda Rhimes, Naval Ravikant, Brian Koppelman, Howard Marks, James Clear, Peter Diamandis, Dan Sullivan, and more, and wanted to figure out what made them different.

The answer: they took responsibility for the results in their life.

Now, let's look at one way you can take responsibility for your life: your calendar.

RPM Planning for Creatives

Tony's signature productivity program that he teaches is known as RPM, or the Rapid Planning Method. RPM also, however, stands for Results-focused, Purpose-driven, Massive action plan. He's getting a lot of mileage out of that acronym . . .

The goal of this productivity system is to help you get the results that matter most and take responsibility for the results in your life and your business. It's not a to-do list. It's not about "getting things done." If you're someone who wants to create, make, or produce—whether it's products, or artwork, or creative projects—this is what RPM is best suited for.

While I can't walk you through every step of the process (get the **tapes** for that) I do want to cover two parts that have played a massive part in my being able to get the results I've mentioned over the last two years. Let's start with the three aspects of the framework, and then how to apply them to your weekly and daily planning.

Results Focused

The biggest shift you'll make using RPM is from thinking about tasks to thinking about results. Tasks are what you do every day, results are what you want long-term.

I don't know about you but I don't get up in the morning excited about a long to-do list. I do, however, get extremely excited about making progress towards the big outcomes that I want in my life. Shifting from "what do I have to do today" to "what do I want to achieve today/this week/this month/this quarter/this year" is massive. It is the first step. You begin by writing down some results you want in both your personal and professional life. Five to seven each is a good number. You did this back in the first part of the book.

If you didn't, take the time now to write them down. These serve as the results that you're going to work towards and that will inform what you choose to do on a daily basis.

Purpose Driven

Once you've got your list of results you want to achieve, and before you start diving into action, we need to add in one extra step. Not for arbitrary reasons. But because the difference between those that get a ton done and accomplish their goals is rarely because of how hard they work. It's the purpose behind the goals that drive them to continue on.

With each one of the results that you've written down, take a few minutes to write down the reasons that the result is important to you.

Some questions may help:

- What will it mean to get this result?
- What will you become when you reach this result?
- What will this help you do?
- Who will it serve?

List out as many reasons that can inform the purpose behind the goal.

Only then can we shift into taking action.

Massive Action

Big goals are achieved by taking the appropriate level of action. Just today I had a phone call with someone who was asking me about what it would take to 10x my business—10x more leads, 10x more value per customer, and 10x more revenue.

I was surprised that it wasn't going to require 10x more action. It wasn't going to take 10x more time. It mainly requires thinking 10x bigger. Thinking about leverage. Thinking about the people you work with and the systems that are working in the background.

Massive action doesn't always mean more time or more effort. It is more of a shift in mindset. What this looks like is listing out all the different ideas that will help you get closer to the result that you're after. This is where we can look at a weekly and daily practice of implementing this RPM system for your creative life and business.

Weekly RPM Planning Session

Each week, take thirty to sixty minutes to revisit your goals and the results that matter to you. Make any additions or take out any that aren't serving you anymore or have been achieved.

Look at the results that you want to accomplish and pick a few that are most important to you for the week ahead. Add to your list of reasons and expand the purpose that's driving you to get those results. Then write down all the big actions you can take this week to get that result.

Do this step for each result that you want to work towards this week.

Then, to take it one step further, roughly map out your week. Pick a day or a block of time during the week that you can devote to that result. I've found it more effective to put all the actions for one result into as few chunks as possible, rather than work on every result every day of the week.

Being able to go deep on something each day will get you more progress than spreading those tasks over the whole week. Try to get one or two blocks of a few hours into your schedule for the week. Getting them into your schedule or calendar before the week starts will prevent other tasks or invitations from holding back your progress.

This is when you take control of your time. If you have your week scheduled before it starts, you're by default not available for last-minute meetings or random requests. This raises the bar for the things that do pop up—they better be good to replace what you've already scheduled for your week.

Here's what my calendar for the week generally looks like on Sunday night, before the week starts:

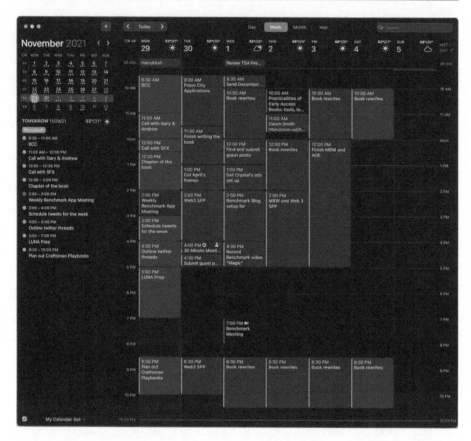

Fully booked! Want to schedule time with me? You'll have to schedule it next week.

Daily RPM Planning

Each day—and it doesn't matter if it's first thing in the morning, or at the end of the day in preparation for the next day—take fifteen to twenty minutes to revisit your plan for the week and get more detail on the work you want to do for the day.

Schedule when you're going to work on your project. Write down the people you need to communicate or follow up with. List out any other actions that will help you get the result you're after.

I've started using Roam Research for this (in the past I've used both Evernote and Notion, but have landed on Roam as my current favorite in the last year), in conjunction with a physical planner. I get up early and do my morning routine, and then fifteen minutes of RPM planning this **physical planner**.

When I start working, I put my tasks from the planner into Roam so that it lives on my second computer screen all day. I can then tick off the tasks that I've accomplished and capture new ideas or tasks throughout the day, and then more easily copy & paste anything that needs to be done tomorrow if I didn't get to it today.

The Results Speak for Themselves

Remember our three personas? It's where we began this journey together, and it's where I'd like to end it as well. After all, it's only by wearing those three hats that we can reach our ultimate goal of moving from a five-figure creator to a flourishing, six-figure business owner. How you show up in your business is such a huge determinant of your success both now and in the future.

So, step into your Manager persona for a minute now. Embrace the systems and the calendar scheduling and the optimization part of your brain! Schedule into your calendar one day every year and every quarter for your Entrepreneur to show up and have a day where they are in control of your business. Look at and adjust your vision. Set goals. Dream big dreams. Capture them in a way that your Manager can then create plans to hand off to the Artist.

Next, schedule one day per month (generally the first day or first Monday of each month) for your Manager to take the reins and outline the plan to achieve the goals set by the Entrepreneur for the quarter.

Lastly, clear some space for the Artist to do the work every day, uninterrupted, to create amazing work. Make sure that you reserve time for that deep, creative work. If you try and fit it in "whenever you can," you'll see that the other parts of your life and business expand to fill the time, so the very first thing you should add to your calendar every day is a nice one to four hour block of creative time where you can shut off the world and do that creative work that your business is built on.

Remember, without a product, you have no business. Without a manager, your business won't operate smoothly, and you'll find yourself stressed and frustrated. And without an entrepreneur taking the reins every so often your business will never grow beyond what your artist and manager can do on their own.

When you're constantly reviewing your high-level goals and results for your life and business, you can't help but focus on them and make progress. Exciting goals turn into exciting days working towards them.

Whatever system you choose, the important principles are to focus on the outcomes first and let the tasks be determined within that context, and to revisit your goals and results often to not only measure them but to keep them top of mind.

My hope is that this chapter inspires you to take responsibility for the results you're getting in your life and business.

Life doesn't owe you anything. Your industry and your market don't owe you anything. As much as you want to succeed, you've got to take responsibility for the results you're getting now, and the results you want in the future.

Try this system if you don't already have a productivity system that's delivering the results you want. Tweak it. Make it yours. Identify the constraints in your business and take action. With a long-term approach to your success, doing more of what works and less of what doesn't, over time you're all but guaranteed to succeed.

Conclusion

Your Creative Projects

At the beginning of this book, I mentioned that I wasn't going to cover the process of doing creative work or creating projects.

The reason is two-fold:

The process is different for everyone.

You have to consider temperament, personality, time of day, and so many other things, that writing that book or trying to prescribe a singular process was too big an undertaking for this book.

I'd already created a course on the topic.

Last year, when I started Craftsman Creative, I hadn't yet learned the importance of building an audience first. I came out the gate with two of my own courses. The first was about doing creative work at a professional level.

It covers how to align your creative work with who you are as an artist and creator, how to do it at a professional level, and provides a proven framework for creative projects. You can find it at craftsmancreative.co/courses/make-something. And if you use the code **buddypass** at checkout, you get 10 percent off, since you already purchased this book!

I hope you enjoy the course. And I hope you can take what you've learned from this book to grow a truly great creative life and business.

Go Deeper With The Craftsman Creative Courses

Along with this book I launched a new online course by the same name. It is a more visual way to learn the principles and frameworks I cover in the book. If you're looking for more depth than a book can provide, or want to learn in a different way to better cement these new habits and lessons into your life, then check out the course at craftsmancreative.co.

There is also a live, cohort-based course launching along with the book that will repeat one or two times a year. You can learn about that at craftsmancreative.co as well if you'd like the added benefit of learning with a group of creators on the same path as you, want personal attention and feedback on your creative business, and want the accountability and compression of a live course.

Continuing Your Journey Toward Mastery

My hope with this book is that it is a starting point, not an end to your creative journey. I feel privileged to have been able to join you as a companion on the path. Making it this far in the book says something about you—that you're determined, that you're serious, that you are resilient, and that you desire the change that this book promises.

It means that you're my kind of person.

Consider this a special invitation.

An invite to a society of independent creators. A group of artists and makers and founders and developers and musicians and entrepreneurs, just like you, who want a place not only to share and showcase their work, but to . . .

. . . continue their journey toward mastery

. . . build resilient, profitable businesses

. . . connect with like-minded creators

. . . continue their journey with people who are on the same path as them

This invitation won't last forever. If that kind of a group sounds exciting to you, I hope you'll join us.

You can learn more and sign up at societyofindependentcreators.com

A Special Invitation for the 1 Percent

My experience has taught me that in any audience I've ever connected with, there's generally 1 percent of people who really "get it." Some people call that 1 percent your **True Fans**. I like how that sounds. You're true. You're proven. You're different from the rest.

You're here.

But an even smaller number of you reading these very words right now, those of you who have made it this far, still feel some tension created by this book.

That tension was intentional, and it's a way to identify those "true fans."

You want something more. You want more connection, more access, more certainty that all of the principles and frameworks can be applied in your own life and that you can have the success you want.

So, this invitation is for you.

I have a few ways that you can work with me. From coaching to consulting to courses and more, there are a myriad of ways that I can join you on your creative journey and help you get where you want to go.

I do limit the amount of coaching and consulting work that I do to only four clients at a time. But if you'd like to work with me, you can visit this link to learn more, or email me directly here.

I can't wait to hear from you and to discover who you are.

Special Thanks

There were so many people integral to the creation of this book. Let's start from the beginning:

My wife April, for always being so supportive of all of my different creative projects. I certainly couldn't do all of this without her, and she has the greatest ability to lift people up and make them feel like they can take on the world. She's also a world-class photographer: https://bladhphotography.com

Rob Fitzpatrick (@robfitz) wrote the book that inspired the writing of this book. His book, Write Useful Books and community and friendship have been such a huge benefit as I've gone through this whole process.

Joe Pulizzi (@joepulizzi) is another author who's writing led to the idea of this book. His most recent book Content Inc. inspired me to think of my business in a whole new way, and to think of myself as a content entrepreneur, not just a content creator. He's also helped guide me through the world of web3, and much of the NFT/Creator Coin/etc parts of this book launch can be traced back to him sharing his learnings with his Tilt community.

Kevon Cheung (@meetkevon) was an early connection made through Rob's community, and was a huge support and early feedback-giver. He's truly a giver, as you'll see when you follow him online. He's helping creators grow in a sustainable way and his content is so pure and good.

Mark Modesti (@markmodesti) was one of the earliest beta-readers, ever willing to give feedback on early chapters of the book. Thank you so much, Mark!

Brian Clark (@brianclark) and Jerod Morris (@jerodmorris) have been a guiding light in the creator economy over this last year. Their content, community, education on web3, and history of teaching creators has been truly inspirational, and they've been willing to connect and share at a moment's notice.

Samantha Demers (@samanthademers) has become a dear friend - and hopefully a future collaborator. One of the first Twitter friends who I've been able to meet up with "in real life", she is truly inspirational in the realm of audience building and inspiring creators online.

Alexandre Philippe (@alexbuddyup1) is another creator I met through Rob's community, and was so willing to hop on a call and give feedback in the earliest stages of my book. His willingness to give his time and his feedback helped set the book on a solid path.

Sam Holstein (samholstein.com) gave some incredible, honest feedback early on that made me take a deeper look at the intention behind my writing, and to take a look at my writing style. Sam is an incredible writer as well, so head to the website to check it out!

Stacey Gonzales (@staceypacer) has become a friend over these last few months, and her early support and encouragement helped me see that I was on the right path and that the book was going to help people. You can see an early exchange of ours in the book!

Aprilynne Alter (@aprilynnea) is a brilliant designer and content creator. She designed my Twitter banner (as an NFT that I was quick to acquire!) and has been a big help in framing my content on Twitter to help reach more people.

Dylan Redekop (@growthcurrency) helped promote my book chapters early on, and we've since become friends online. His willingness to help and support the book have been much-needed when I doubted that the book would ever resonate with an audience.

Josh Spector (@jspector) is a consummate creator and one of my favorite people to follow on Twitter. His ability to distill knowledge and information has helped me frame my writing for the book, and his early support in sharing a chapter in his newsletter helped propel the awareness of the book in ways I never expected.

Arvid Kahl (@arvidkahl) is another friend met through Rob's community and on Twitter, and I finally got the chance to chat with him on Twitter Spaces just before the book launch. We see the creator economy very similarly, and he's been a huge support in helping promote the book.

Justin Moore (@justinmooretfam) is an incredible friend and support, and has said "Yes!" to basically anything I've asked whether it be support with sponsorships, or coming on Twitter Spaces, or promoting my book in his (must-read) newsletter. He's a friend for life and is similarly passionate about helping creators succeed in their businesses.

Last, but not least - while this book is dedicated to my wife and our three "dudes", I want to thank my Grandfather, Edward Lindsay Carlisle, who passed away last year just before I started working on this book. He has been a life-long supporter of me and my creative pursuits, and the last time I talked to him was a tear-filled chat at his bed-side where he told me how proud of me he was for achieving everything I wanted in my creative life. I felt his hand at times during the process of writing this book, and have been inspired by his love for his family and willingness to serve and help others. I hope this book can be a testament to that legacy, and that it has even a fraction of the impact on your life, as he has had on mine.